HARRY PECKHAM'S
TOUR

T0323311

HARRY PECKHAM'S
TOUR

EDITED BY MARTIN BRAYNE

The
History
Press

Front cover: *Harry Peckham* (oil on canvas), Joseph Wright of Derby, *c.* 1762. Private Collection

Back cover: *General View of the Chateau and Pavilions at Marly, 1722* (oil on canvas), by Martin, Pierre-Denis (1663–1742) © Chateau de Versailles, France/Giraudon/The Bridgeman Art Library

First published in 1772
This edition published by Nonsuch Publishing in 2008, reprinted 2020

Nonsuch Publishing is an imprint of The History Press Limited

97 St George's Place, Cheltenham,
www.thehistorypress.co.uk

British Library Cataloguing in Publication Data:
A catalogue record for this book is available from the British Library

ISBN 978 1 84588 619 6

Typesetting and origination by The History Press
Printed and bound in Great Britain by TJ International Ltd, Padstow, Cornwall.

Contents

Illustrations

Harry Peckham's Bookplate, West Sussex Record Office.

Harry Peckham, (oil on canvas), Joseph Wright of Derby, *c*.1762, Private Collection.

The Young Bull, (oil on canvas) by Potter, Paulus (1625–54) © Mauritshuis, The Hague, Netherlands/The Bridgeman Art Library.

Bibliotheca Thysiana, Leiden—Photograph: Pepicek.

Ghent-Bruges Draw Barge, by kind permission of Cambridge Antiquarian Society.

Lille, Porte de Paris, Editor's Collection.

Christ on the Cross, *c*.1628-30 (oil on canvas) by Dyck, Sir Anthony van (1599-1641) © Musée des Beaux-Arts, Lille, France/Lauros/Giraudon/The Bridgeman Art Library.

Lille, Citadelle, Editor's Collection.

A Street Scene in Paris (La Parade du Boulevard), 1760 (oil on canvas) by Saint-Anton, Gabriel Jacques de (1724-80) © National Gallery, London, UK/The Bridgeman Art Library.

The Birth of Louis XIII (1601-43) at Fontainebleau, 27ᵗʰ September 1601, from the Medici Cycle, 1621-25, (oil on canvas) by Rubens © Louvre, Paris, France/Lauros/Giraudon/The Bridgeman Art Library.

View of the Chapel of the Chateau de Versailles from the Courtyard, (oil on canvas) by Rigaud, Jacques (1681-1754) (after) © Chateau de Versailles, France/Giraudon/ The Bridgeman Art Library.

General View of the Chateau and Pavilions at Marly, 1722 (oil on canvas) by Martin, Pierre-Denis (1663-1742) © Chateau de Versailles, France/Giraudon/The Bridgeman Art Library.

Introduction

When in 1807 Robert Southey, purporting to be a Spanish gentleman, wrote the preface to his *Letters from England*, he began:

> A volume of travels rarely or never, in our days, appears in Spain: in England, on the contrary, scarcely any works are so numerous. If an Englishman spends the summer in any of the mountainous provinces, or runs over to Paris for six weeks, he publishes the history of his travels …[1]

The present book is a good example of the genre to which Southey referred. It was originally published in 1772 under a typically overweight eighteenth century title—*The Tour of Holland, Dutch Brabant, the Austrian Netherlands and Parts of France: in which is included a Description of Paris and its Environs.* In common with many travel books of its time it took epistolary form; a device made famous by the French Huguenot François-Maximilian Misson whose *Nouveau Voyage d'Italie* had been published in The Hague in 1691 and translated into English four years later. Greatly admired by Joseph Addison, Misson's book was much imitated. One of the most successful books of the type, Patrick Brydone's *Tour through Sicily and Malta in a series of letters addressed to William Beckford,* was published in the year following the appearance of Peckham's *Tour.*

Self-effacement was another frequently adopted authorial ploy, designed to stress that the writer was a gentleman and not a Grub Street hack scratching away in a garret. Edmund Bott, Peckham's exact contemporary, declared that his book, *The Excursion to Holland and the German Spa 1767,* 'must not be dignified with the magnificent title of *Travels.* A lounge it might very properly be called, as it was undertaken without any hope of instruction to the traveller himself or of utility to his country but for the gratification of his curiosity and for that alone'.[2] Harry Peckham insisted that his letters 'cannot do their author credit' so that he was obliged to insist upon 'my name being concealed'.

Although the book turned out to be a considerable commercial success, running eventually to five editions, its author remained anonymous until the fourth appeared in 1788 when he was revealed to be—

> the late Harry Peckham Esq.
> One of His Majesty's Council and
> Recorder of the City of Chichester

Christened Harry, not as some have assumed Henry, Peckham was the son of the Reverend Henry Peckham of Amberley, Sussex, later Rector of Tangmere, near Chichester. Henry was a kinsman of Henry 'Lisbon' Peckham, the builder of grandiose Pallant House in Chichester.[3] A striking feature of the house is the stone birds on the gate piers; intended as ostriches, their appearance gave rise to the nick-name 'The Dodo House'. The ostrich appears on the crest of the Peckham family's arms and can be seen on Harry's bookplate.

Educated at Winchester and New College, Oxford, of which he was a Fellow from 1761 until his death in 1787 at the age of 46, Peckham was called to the Bar in 1767, became King's Counsel and bencher in 1782, died in his chambers in the Middle Temple and was buried in the Temple Church. At the time of his death he was Steward of New College, one of His Majesty's Commissioners for Bankrupts and, as we have seen, Recorder of Chichester.

Harry Peckman was thus a successful lawyer but by no means a famous one, so that, whilst most of the principal events of his existence are not difficult to trace, it is harder to put flesh on the biographical bones. His book, of course, helps, revealing as it does a man of tireless energy and strong—if not always original—opinion. We know something of his physical appearance, for at about the time he graduated he had his portrait painted by the up-and-coming Joseph Wright of Derby. It is a swagger portrait typical of the day, so whether he was quite so handsome or cut quite so dashing a figure we must doubt. He does seem to think rather highly of himself.

The portrait is one of six painted by Wright for Francis Noel Clarke Mundy of Markeaton Hall, Derbyshire; they are of himself and five sporting friends. Mundy was a contemporary of Peckham's at New College where he was a gentleman-commoner. Such students were invariably from rich families and were admitted in the expectation that they would prove to be, in the fullness of time, generous benefactors.[4] The pictures were painted shortly after Mundy inherited Markeaton and each of the young sparks is shown wearing the distinctive livery of the private Markeaton Hunt.[5] Although not averse to excessive drinking, Mundy was no Squire Western.[6] He was also a poet, most famously the author of *Needwood Forest* (1776) and, after enclosure, *The Fall of Needwood* (1808). He was to become a member of the distinguished Lichfield literary circle which included Erasmus Darwin, Sir Brooke Boothby, Richard Lovell Edgeworth and Anna Seward.[7]

That the rakishness suggested by Peckham's portrait had some substance in the man himself finds support both in the *Tour* and elsewhere in the written record. The *Tour* hints at a youngish man—he was 29 when it was undertaken—with an eye for the ladies; be it the 'young, sprightly and handsome' daughter of his Parisian landlord or the nude subject of a Titian painting or the celebrated statue of the Venus aux Belles Fesses in the garden at Marly-le-Roi. More conclusive evidence of the sowing of wild oats is to be found in his Will, drawn up on the 29 December 1784.[8] Firstly, there is the French snuff box 'with a saucy picture set in gold' which he gives to a Chichester friend. Then there are some matters which must have weighed more heavily on the testator's mind. We discover that he bequeathed an annuity of sixty pounds to Sarah Thompson, widow, and daughter of John Cooper of St Martin's le Grand, London, as recompense 'for an injury which many years since I attempted to do her'. We also find that his principal beneficiary was his daughter Sarah 'born the third of May seventeen hundred and seventy one'. This despite the fact that nowhere, either in the Will or elsewhere, is a wife mentioned. One explanation, however, certainly presents itself; as a fellow of an Oxford college he was expected to be celibate and upon marriage his fellowship would have been automatically rescinded. We must assume either that he married in secret or that Sarah was born out of wedlock. Clearly he concealed, but did not deny, paternity. Alas, the Will was still the subject of a case in Chancery twenty years after Peckham's death; the heirs of his executors fighting over their share of the spoils.[9]

We have another source of information which helps to fill out our picture of the author of the *Tour*. James Woodforde was another contemporary of Peckham. Born in the same year—1740—he too was educated at Winchester and New College. From shortly before going up to Oxford in the autumn of 1759 until a few months before he died in 1803, Woodforde kept a diary fascinating not as a record of great men and events, for he became a country clergyman, but for the remarkable wealth of quotidian detail of eighteenth-century life which it preserves. Peckham makes his first appearance in Woodforde's diary—best known as *The Diary of a County Parson*—shortly after going up to Oxford when, on 6 October 1759 'Geree, Peckham & myself had a Hogshead of Port from Mr Cropp at Southampton.'[10] How long it took the three students to consume the 57 imperial gallons which a hogshead comprised we cannot be sure, but Woodforde's *Diary* suggests not very long.

In general the two undergraduates probably rubbed along pretty well together. Woodforde lent Peckham his 'great coat and black Cloth Waistcoat'[11] to go to Henley Assembly and, when the diarist was confined to his college rooms with an attack of boils, Peckham and another student 'had their Suppers here and spent the Evening with me'.[12] On the day after they had both obtained their fellowships they went, together with two others, to London. They visited Vauxhall, which Peckham in the *Tour* was to compare with a pleasure garden of the same name in Paris and, in the evening, they went to the Theatre Royal, Drury Lane, to see *All in the Wrong*, a new play by Samuel Johnson's friend Arthur Murphy.[13] As we shall see, Peckham had a keen interest in the stage and in his book was to make illuminating comparisons between London theatres and those of The Hague, Amsterdam, Brussels, Lille and Paris.

However, although they often drank, gambled and played together, the relationship between future parson and future lawyer seems to have found expression in rivalry as often as in comradeship. On one occasion Peckham, a keen sportsman, 'laid me that his first Hands at Crickett was better than Bennett Snr's and he was beat',[14] but on another—

> Peckham walked round the Parks for a Wager this Morning: he walked round the Parks three times in 26 Minutes, being 2 miles and a Quarter. Williams and myself laid him a Crown that he did not do it in 30 Minutes and we lost our Crown by four minutes. I owe Peckham for Walking—0:2:6[15]

Although Woodforde sometimes had sharp words for fellow collegians he is rarely quite as critical as he is of Harry Peckham whose energy and ambition the somewhat slothful diarist may well have envied. He made no particular objection when the barrister-to-be sconced (i.e. fined) him, two bottles of wine 'for throwing' in the Bachelors' Common Room[16] but when they argued against one another in the Latin disputation which formed part of the degree examination, Woodforde dismissed his opponent's arguments as 'very low, paultry and false'[17]. At a later date, when Peckham's position as Senior Collector required him to make a speech in the Sheldonian Theatre before the Vice Chancellor, the highly conventional Woodforde described it as 'very indifferent … being of his own composing.'[18] But by this time their friendship had certainly cooled. On 1 June 1763 they had both, together with a number of other New College men, taken their BA degree. As was customary they had treated the other members of the College to wine and punch. Woodforde, usually no slouch when it came to the circulating bottle and the punchbowl, had stayed up until mid-night and had then retired to his room but at three in the morning, he subsequently complained to his Diary—

> had my outward Doors broken open, my Glass Doors broke, and [was] pulled out of bed and brought to the BCR where I was obliged to drink and smoak, but not without a good many words—Peckham broke my Doors, being very drunk altho' they were open, which I do not relish of Mr Peckham much—[19]

Peckham was not, of course, the first drunken vandal in university history and was certainly not the last but his action that night probably ensured that James Woodforde would not be one of the two friends with whom at the end of July six years later Peckham set off on his continental tour.[20]

At a later date the undergraduate body at Oxford was divided, stereotypically at least, between boisterous, sports-playing, champagne-drinking 'hearties' and limp-wristed, poetry-reading 'aesthetes'. Although, as we have seen, Harry Peckham had more than a little of the 'hearty' about him, the *Tour* reveals that he was by no means a philistine. Whilst his taste in architecture, painting, gardening and sculpture was conventional, it was neither uninformed nor unintelligent. He was neither a great connoisseur—the works of which he approved were rarely other than 'fine', 'admirable' or 'magnificent'—nor a 'grand milord' buying-up all that he could irrespective of quality. Thus in painting he is dismissive of 'mere mannerism' but is always happy to be deceived by a well-executed *trompe d'oeil* such as the 'Game-piece' by Pieter Snyers he sees in Brussels—'in which is a hedge-hog, alive I believe, but I am afraid to satisfy my doubts by the touch, lest it should prick my finger.' In Paris he visited the 1769 *Salon* but was unable to recognise the merits of artists as diverse and gifted as Greuze, Drouais and Hubert Robert for whilst 'In the choice of their subjects there is much imagination … their colours are glaring and instead of nature you have only the tinsel of art.' He lacked the sophistication of Horace Walpole, the individuality of William

Beckford and the perspicacity of Arthur Young yet the very ordinariness of his observations, tells us much about mid-eighteenth-century taste, whilst the practicality of his advice and relentlessness of his curiosity render Peckham's *Tour* both instructive and enjoyable. Whether he visits Versailles or an Amsterdam brothel, travels by *treckschuyte* in Holland or stage coach in Normandy, he takes us along with him on what was not so much a grand tour as a modest, but highly entertaining, excursion. It lasted just nine weeks.

The particular merit of Peckham's *Tour* is that whilst, like Thomas Nugent's *The Grand Tour*, it was clearly intended as a guidebook—containing information on routes, the cost of travel, inns and the sights to be seen—it also included much that is anecdotal and personal. Whilst Nugent's book was aimed at wealthy young men, accompanied by an older governor or 'bearleader', the point of whose travelling was 'to enrich the mind with knowledge, to rectify the judgment, to remove the prejudices of education, to compare the outward manners and, in a word, to form the complete gentleman', Peckham and his friends travelled for pleasure and set off hoping to 'blunder through the country as well as we can without other assistance than a little French and some money'.[21]

Although eighteenth-century Oxford was a stronghold of Toryism, Peckham's sympathies, as revealed in the *Tour,* are of a decidedly Whiggish cast.[22] Thus protestant, capitalist Holland is seen in a generally favourable light; the struggle for independence from Catholic Spain being treated with particular admiration. This is not to say that all things Dutch receive a seal of approval—their language, for example, 'even from the mouth of a beauty would be an antidote to venery'. Clean, well-dressed, hard-working and ingenious, the contrast between the inhabitants of the United Provinces and the French, whose good qualities 'are confined in very narrow compass', could hardly be more stark. Of the latter he asserts 'Their religion seems calculated for the vulgar, and is rather to amuse than to amend', whilst all but those who can afford to pay—the aristocracy and the clergy, who are excused—are burdened with an oppressive system of taxation in order to support a tyrannical monarchy. Had he lived to be fifty, the Revolution would have come as no more of a surprise to Harry Peckham than it did to Arthur Young.[23]

What he could never have imagined was the degree of disruption which the Revolution and the subsequent wars would bring about. Many of the abbeys, churches and palaces he had strolled around on the tour would not survive into the new century. Bronzes would be melted down for cannon and art collections dispersed. Had he reached the age of 70 and once again wished to admire Paulus Potter's painting *The Young Bull*, he would have had to travel not to The Hague, where he had seen it in 1769, but to the Louvre where it formed part of Napoleon's vast cultural trophy bag. In 1815 many of the Emperor's ill-gotten gains would be repatriated but no such happy outcome awaited the countless families bereaved by sabre thrust, musket ball and guillotine. The *Tour* pictures a world soon to be irretrievably changed.

On his return from the tour Peckham, like a friend who lives a long way from us, is seen only occasionally. In the summer of 1771 we glimpse him on Broadhalfpenny Down, a member of the Sussex cricket team which defeated the Gentlemen of Hampshire. Three years later he was one of the Committee of Noblemen and Gentlemen who codified the laws of the game.[24] As in his student days, when he had gravitated towards the wealthy gentlemen-commoners, he was quite clearly moving in socially elevated circles; the Committee included the Duke of Dorset and a sprinkling of knights.

Later in 1774 he was one of the Sussex freeholders who, unhappy with the performance of their sitting M.P., Richard Harcourt, refused to endorse his candidature and, wishing to break the power of the Pelhams in the county, persuaded the reluctant Sir Thomas Spencer Wilson to stand. Peckham, in striking contrast to Wilson, threw himself into the campaign, bombarding the candidate with information and advice. His motive seems not to have been personal gain for not only did the freeholders make voluntary subscriptions to support the cause but Sir Thomas made clear that he 'would not be at any expense, either in carrying, supporting or ornamenting any voter, or on any other account, except the legal expenses of the poll'.[25] From London Peckham sent exuberant, hastily-written bulletins full of news of how badly Wilson's rival, Sir James Peachey, was faring—'I have seen since I left you every symptom of a dying party making their last efforts'—and of reassurances about the cost of the election—'If your Election continues till Wednesday you will have saved above a 100gns'. 'Go and prosper!' he urged the unenthusiastic baronet.[26] Wilson's total election expenses amounted to £720, a very modest sum for a contested election at a time when bribery and lavish entertainment was the norm.[27] His success was doubtless far more welcome to Peckham than to the half-hearted new Member.[28]

In the following year Peckham was himself an election candidate. The post of Steward of New College fell vacant and Peckham put his name forward. Woodforde decided to vote for him on grounds of convention—'his Application being first'—rather than friendship or suitability to the task.[29] The matter was decided on 14 December when, the diarist records:

We had one of the fullest Meetings I think I ever saw in the Hall to day on the Stewards Affair. The first question on the same was whether the Future Steward should keep his Fellowship or not, which after many learned Arguments being Advanced pro & con it passed in the Affirmative—

This decision persuaded Peckham's opponent to withdraw and 'Peckham was declared to be the Steward and received his Patent for the same'.[30] He was clearly happy to retain his fellowship even though it meant keeping quiet about the existence of his daughter, born four years before.

Harry Peckham's legal career reached a climax in 1781 when he was a member of the defence team in the Old Bailey trial of the Frenchman François Henri de la Motte. De la Motte was accused of communicating Royal Navy dispositions to the French allies of the American rebels. During the course of the trial the leading defence barrister was taken ill and Peckham was handed the awful responsibility of summing up in a case in which guilt meant being hung, drawn and quartered. Despite his best efforts the jury were out for a mere eight minutes before bringing in a verdict of guilty. The following year he became a King's Counsel.[31]

The last time Woodforde saw Peckham was in April 1784 when the Warden of New College accompanied, writes the diarist, by 'Peckham the Steward and Jeffries & Jeanes the Outriders' went on a 'Progress'—essentially a tour of inspection—of the College's properties in East Anglia. Woodforde whose parish of Weston Longville was just 8 miles from Norwich met them at the Swan Inn in that city:

> … soon after Tea I went To them & there supped & spent the Evening with them. They were very glad indeed to see me & so was I them.[32]

Except for the Warden 'who looks thin and had a bad Cold & a Cough', they all looked 'pretty well'. The following day Woodforde gave his friends a conducted tour of the city—Castle Hill, the Cathedral, the Bishop's Palace and St Andrew's Hall—sightseeing which surely would have pleased Peckham. In the afternoon they dined upon 'a nice Dish of Fish, Rump of beef boiled, a Veal Cutlet, forced balls, a Turkey roasted & some Lemon Cream'.

On that convivial note we leave Harry Peckham until we rediscover him later in the same year at the solemn business of writing his Will. His youthful excesses behind him, he was clearly anxious to ensure that, posthumously, his responsibilities were discharged. He remained, however, a sportsman to the end; he died in his rooms in the Temple after breaking his neck in a hunting accident. Quite probably it was the journey back to London which killed him. His lively, forceful and ambitious nature would be more faithfully reflected in his *Tour* than in the very modest epitaph—for 'Ostentatious Monuments meet not with my Approbation'—beneath his parents' memorial in Chichester cathedral.[33]

The first edition of Peckham's book is here introduced in its entirety. Original spelling has been retained, only obvious errors being altered. Punctuation has occasionally been modernised to clarify meaning. The footnotes are Peckham's own. Later editions of the book, published after the author's death, contain material, allegedly by 'a Gentleman of Groningen', inserted for purely commercial reasons (containing reference, for example, to places that Peckham did not himself visit). This is of little value to the modern reader and has not been included.

* * * * *

Harry Peckam has for the last four years been an agreeable, if somewhat opinionated, companion. In the course of editing his *Tour* I have introduced him to many friends, acquaintances and complete strangers whose help I have sought and who, without exception, have obliged with their expertise. I would mention in particular Dick Ayres, Pat Creamer, Roy Creamer, Keith Haughan and Peter Searby who have all read and commented helpfully upon parts of the work-in-progress; Aurélien André, the Diocesan Archivist of Amiens; Nicole Backus; Anneke Bakker of the Frans Hals Museum, Haarlem; Penelope Carter of the National Gallery of Scotland; Dick Claessen; Mike Eagles; Matthew Edwards of Derby Art Gallery; Aart van der Houwen; Timothy McCann, formerly of West Sussex Record Office; Noel S. McFerran of Jacobite Heritage; Roy Miles; Ann Raia; Jennifer Thorp, Archivist of New College, Oxford; and H.D. Wessels of the City Archives, Breda. I am especially grateful to Dick Bateman for putting my 'O' Level Latin and much else to shame and Keith Haughan for placing his encyclopaedic knowledge of eighteenth-century French culture at my disposal. Most of all I want to thank Ann, my fellow traveller in the footsteps of Peckham; a happy detour on the journey we share.

Letter I

Dear Sir,

You have sacrificed your judgment to your friendship, or you would not have asked my permission to publish these letters I sent you from abroad, nor endeavoured by compliments to win my consent.

Consider the hasty manner in which they were written; frequently at table, and in the company of my friends; both language and grammar therefore, I am afraid, have often been violated and I have neither time to polish the one, nor inclination to correct the other. The observations are too thinly scattered, and are either crude or common; even the *purpureus pannus* is wanting to recommend them.[34]

You tell me they prove of infinite service to you: because the names and values of the different coins were ascertained and compared with the English: that the distance from place to place with the mode and expense of travelling, was accurately calculated, and none of the places within the tour worthy of a stranger's attention were omitted.[35] I confess that these are advantages to the few who travel, but to other readers will prove only a dry detail.

I have not the vanity to suppose that such letters can benefit either the publisher or the public. I am convinced that they cannot do their author credit, must therefore insist upon my name being concealed, and that you will erase every sentence that might lead to the detection of

Your ever affectionate friend.............[36]

Letter II

Dear Sir,

Nothing could have added to the pleasure I promised myself in this little excursion, but the addition of your company; as the pursuits you are engaged in render it impossible, I must submit, and console myself with endeavouring to make my letters a faithful guide, though not an agreeable companion. As I write with this view, I must often be very tedious in mentioning a thousand little nothings which in your intended tour will not be wholly immaterial, as I know not of any treatise to guide you through Holland, and instruct you in these articles, which every traveller must otherwise be at a loss to know.

After having hunted all the booksellers shops and stalls in London, I at length picked up a voluminous octavo in English, whose title promised me a Description of Holland, with the whole et caetera of manners and customs;—but this pompous *Title* afforded me only a tedious detail of the Hague; we must therefore blunder through the country as well as we can, without other assistance than a little French and some money.[37]

I left London at four in the morning with my two friends, and an English servant who knows no language but his own. The road is well calculated for expedition, being free from hills, and there is but little sand to retard a carriage. We breakfasted at Witham, where there was nothing to attract our attention, but the very great civility of our host at the Blue Posts. We made some little stay at Colchester, to take a cursory view of the town, which is considerable in the number, as well as the goodness of the houses. The grand street is very spacious, on the left of which is an old quadrangular brick castle, converted now into a prison, the only use it can be adapted to.[38] The road does not abound in views, but between Manningtree and Harwich, there are some scenes tolerably picturesque, which are heightened by the tide river which divides Essex and Suffolk.[39]

Harwich is, I think, the worst of all possible places, but the accommodation at the White Hart perhaps made me peevish; add to this, the shoal of scoundrels who pick your pocket with impunity.[40] As it is a borough town, the voters must be provided for, and are rewarded with salaries arising from the fees of such emigrants as myself.

We were first attacked by a clerk for thirteen shillings and sixpence each, for which he generously gave us a piece of paper, which he called a permit, and which was of no other use but for a Dutchman to light his pipe with. He told me, in answer to my inquiry into the nature of his demand, that he was rather thick of hearing; I thought his reason conclusive, and we paid him his fees immediately.

The officers of the customs then insisted on their fees for tumbling our clothes, and deranging our trunks, and for what they called *Sufferance*, which is, "to permit a man to take out of the kingdom what the laws have not prohibited". Having thus run the gauntlet of imposition, we set sail in the Prince of Orange, Captain Story, at half past six in the evening. This vessel carries twelve men, and her burthen is one hundred and six tons. We found excellent accommodations, the cabin being a spacious room and rather elegantly fitted up. The passage must be difficult and extremely dangerous to men not perfectly conversant with these seas, on account of the innumerable shoals and rocks. We were very fortunate in the fineness of the evening, and fairness of the wind. I know not a more glorious sight than the sun setting in the waters; and as the night came on, was much pleased with observing the different lighthouses for the direction of pilots, and the waves striking against the prow of the ship. Philosophers have entertained various opinions concerning this luminous appearance; Boyle attributed it to some cosmic law of the terrestrial globe, or at least of the planetary vortex: but Mr Canton, F.R.S. has proved by experiments, as simple as ingenious, that it arises from the putrefaction of the animal substances in the sea.[41] The Captain entertained us with throwing the log line: this is done by a little square piece of wood let down from the stern of the ship, which is tied to a cord wound on a reel, and at equal distances has knots made in it; from the number of knots which run out in a minute (for which purpose there is a minute glass), the sailors compute how many miles the vessel makes in an hour.[42]

In this manner we land-men amused ourselves, till drowsiness warned us to our cabins: these are little boxes within the sides of the ship of sufficient size to hold one person. As there were no sheets, I turned in with my clothes on and slept very soundly till the Captain waked me in the morning, with the pleasing news of our being within sight of Helveot, where we landed about ten o'clock; and as soon as we had refreshed ourselves with a dish of tea, spent the remainder of the day in examining this little sea-port.

Helveotsluice is situated on the island of Voorn, in the province of Holland; is surrounded with a wet fosse and a strong rampart faced with brick; which is intended, as much, I believe, to guard against the irruption of the waves, as of an enemy. The harbour, which seems wonderfully safe, runs through the middle of the town, and projects by the help of piers, about fifty yards into the main ocean. There is grandeur in this attempt, which I should not have thought the Dutch capable of, though I am well aware that their industry would surmount the difficulty. The water at the pier-head is ninety feet deep, the piles are one hundred and forty feet long, and are driven thirty-five feet into the shore, the interstices are filled with Bavins, which are kept down with large stones brought from Norway.[43] The dexterity of our naval charioteer pleased me much, for he turned round the corner of the pier as sharp an angle as I have ever seen made by a carriage.

This harbour is full of ships; on each side is a spacious quay laid with Dutch clinkers beyond which is a façade of houses most whimsically pretty; the window shutters are all painted with yellow or green, and there is a painted bench at every door, where the people sit in stupid inactivity, and I believe without any conversation, for I have scarce seen a mouth open unless to yawn. The houses are built in a wretched style, with narrow fronts, running up to a point, by which means the gable end destroys the attic story.

The harbour runs through the town to a large bason, which contains at present twelve men of war lying in perfect security. It is divided from the harbour by a pair of flood-gates, over which is thrown a bridge of curious mechanism. It divides in the middle, and under the centre of each half are sixteen brass wheels fixed on an axle which stands on a large buttress; it is so nicely hung that a child may turn it, when both parts of the bridge point up and down the harbour, which effectually stops the passage.

In the dock there seems to be but a very inconsiderable quantity of naval stores, and in the barracks, which are extremely neat, only two companies of soldiers. The walks upon the ramparts are very pleasing, being turfed and perfectly clean, as indeed is almost everything here—so nice are they, that at our hostess's, Mrs Wykham's, there is a little scale hangs upon the nose of the boiler to catch the drops lest they should fall upon the hearth, which is of polished stone and I narrowly escaped a beating from the chambermaid for having my hair powdered in my bed chamber. We strolled into a church, which had nothing but cleanliness to recommend it. The men sit with their hats on, and both men and women are seated in the body of the church in chairs numbered on the backs. The priest spoke extempore with fluency but as I know not the language am ignorant of his merit.

The Captain promised to put this letter in the post at Harwich; you shall hear from me again, as soon as I have matter to communicate, and time to write. We purpose leaving this place tomorrow morning.

Adieu!

Letter III

Dear Sir,

We left Helveot on Monday morning in a stage waggon, which was the best conveyance the place afforded; and even to get that requires no little form. I went to the Commissary, who upon receiving six stivers rang a bell, which in a few moments summoned all the waggoners in the town, when thus assembled, to prevent partiality in the Commissary, and disputes among the drivers, the dice determine who shall have the fare, for which purpose there is fixed over the Commissary's door a kind of manger with a large box and dice.[44] The price is fixed, imposition therefore is impossible. This miserable vehicle differs only from an English cart in being somewhat slighter, and by having the cover painted with different colours; it is drawn by a pair of horses, and guided by the boor who sits in the head of it. To this machine there are no shafts, but a piece of wood, like a bugle horn, comes from the axle, with an iron hook, into which the driver puts one foot, and with it guides the carriage to a hair's breadth, the other he claps on the posteriors of one of the horses, in this manner we travelled through very indifferent roads, and at a very modest pace to the Brill; I believe their pace is fixed as their price; and you might as easily persuade one of these savages to accelerate the one as to diminish the other.

The *Brill* is larger than Helveot, and is tolerably fortified; the buildings are old but regular, the streets are spacious, and some of them lined with trees. This town is situated on the mouth of the Maes, which is a mile and a half wide. All the vessels that go to Rotterdam pass by this place; and there is a boat for passengers which sails every tide for Rotterdam. A tolerable trade is still carried on here, but it has dwindled much from its former importance.

This was the first town taken by the malecontents [sic], under the Count of Marche, from the Spaniards in 1572, which was afterwards delivered up to Queen Elizabeth, with Flushing and Ramekins, as a mortgage, for the money she had expended in supporting the states against Philip the second of Spain.[45]

These cautionary towns were given up by James the first, in 1616, for one third of the money they were originally pledged for, owing to the poverty and folly of the king and to the subtilty of the pensionary Barneveldt, who managed the negotiation.[46]

There are twelve companies of soldiers quartered in the town; the Dutch uniform is blue, faced with red, which is not so brilliant in appearance as the English and French uniforms. We attended the parade and were treated with much civility by an officer of the corps who could speak English. The parade being finished, a grenadier was flogged for drunkenness; he received twenty two strokes with the flat of a broadsword over his clothes; a punishment as trifling as with us the offence is common. From the Brill we passed the Maes in a ferry boat to Boors Island, a place of inconsiderable extent, but large enough to sustain six hundred head of cattle, four hundred of which have died within these three months of the distemper, which rages through the whole province with the most fatal violence.[47]

We were shaken over this island in a common cart, the only convenience of the place and crossed another branch of the Maes which brought us to Maesland-sluice, esteemed one of the finest villages in the south part of Holland. It is an extensive place, well-built with canals running through almost every street; those which have not the benefit of the water are ornamented with rows of walnut-trees; and though chiefly inhabited by fishermen, the town is as neat as cleanliness can make it. We stayed here only for the setting out of the Treckschuyte, which goes to Delft six times a day. It resembles a livery barge on the Thames, but is smaller and less ornamented; it is drawn by one horse, and goes with the greatest ease four miles in an hour, which is the Dutch method of computing distance; so many hours to such a place; not leagues like the French, nor miles, as the English.[48] In fine weather this method of travelling is absolutely delightful; for a mere trifle you may hire the *roof*, which is a small cabin at the end of the boat with two sash windows on each side, a table in the middle, velvet cushions to sit on, and good room for six or eight people.[49] The motion of the boat is imperceptible, and you may read, write, eat or sleep, with as much ease as in your own chamber. If this is not agreeable, you may get on top of the boat, which has a flat roof, on which you may walk without danger, and as there is not a hillock in the country, you have nothing to intercept your view. I was almost sorry to leave the treckschuyte which landed us at Delft about five o'clock in the evening. We dined at the Doele, a most admirable inn, and after dinner took a little walk around the city, which is in circumference between two and three miles, of an oblong figure, surrounded by an old wall and ditch, and defended by three dams against inundations. It is situated between Rotterdam and the Hague. The streets are wide, adorned with trees and canals and a multitude of stone bridges: the inhabitants are rich, but being chiefly people who have retired from business, the trade of the place is but inconsiderable; even the Delft manufactory (which is little inferior to China except in transparency; which has been in vain attempted) greatly decays; the Dutch East India Company having imported such quantities of China that it is become within the purchase of the lower class of people.[50]

The principal magazine and armoury of Holland is in the town; which does not make a very formidable appearance.[51] We saw the old palace, which is now inferior to a common burgher's house. They shew you the mark of the balls in the wall which went through the head of the first Prince of Orange, the founder of the state, who was assassinated by Balthazar Ghirard, an emissary of Philip the Second.[52] His tomb is shewn in the New Church, in marble, of very indifferent execution; the epitaph concludes in these words— "Herois veré pii, prudentia, invicti, quem Philippus Secundus Hisp. Rex, Europae timor, timuit, non domuit, non terruit, sed empt percussore, fraude nefandâ sustulit".[53] This church has the finest steeple in the low countries; and the chimes, which play every quarter of an hour, are most unusually harmonious.

In the old church are two monuments erected to the memory of Van Trump and Peter Heine, remarkable only for the heroes they are to perpetuate.[54]

The Market-place is a spacious square; on one side stands the New Church; on the other the Town-house, which in an old Gothic building, but tricked out with paint and ornament, so as to cut no contemptible figure.

The Spin-house, or Bridewell, is as neat as any private house in England. Fornication is not so commendable, I find, in Holland as with us; at least in the eye of the magistracy, for there are many more poor girls confined for their *philanthropy*, for five, ten and some for twenty years.

The two chief streets lie parallel with each other and are near a mile in length— canals run through them edged with stately trees. Before most of the doors is a pavement of black and white marble; but as there is a bench at every house, it effectively prevents any person from walking on such excellent pavement.

About noon on Tuesday we left Delft and took the treckschuyte to this place. The quay we embarked from was very spacious, adorned with trees and the canal broader than I had seen. It is a most agreeable journey to Rotterdam; the number of little gardens and pleasure houses built on the banks of the canal, the little village of Overschie which is about mid-way, and a fine avenue of trees about half a mile in length which leads to the gates of Rotterdam, all conspire to fill the mind with pleasure.

Rotterdam lies on the north side of the Maes, about fifteen miles from the sea, is of a triangular form and, in point of trade, inferior only to Amsterdam; in the spaciousness of the streets and elegance of the houses infinitely beyond it. The canals are so large as to admit ships of two or three hundred tons, even to the very doors of the merchants; and I know not so romantic a sight as to see from the environs, the chimnies, masts of ships and tops of trees so promiscuously huddled together that it would require a degree of divination to tell whether it is a town, a fleet or a forest.

The grandest as well as the most agreeable street in Rotterdam is the Bomb Quay, which lies parallel with the Maes. On one side it lies open to the river and the other is ornamented with a grand façade of the best houses in the city, inhabited chiefly by the English. It is so broad that there are distinct walks for carriages and foot passengers, lined and shaded with a double row of trees.[55] You look over the river on some beautiful meadows and a fine avenue of trees which leads to the Pest-house. It seems to be an elegant building and the trees round it are so dispersed as to appear as a thick wood.

This street is at least half a mile in length and extends from the Old to the New head; the two places where the water enters to fill the various canals of this extensive city. I must observe that when water runs through a street, it assumes the name of a canal; of which kind the Heerenfleet has the pre-eminence. The houses are of free-stone and very lofty. The canal is spacious and covered with ships. At one end stands the English church, a neat, pretty building of which the Bishop of London is Ordinary.[56]

Upon the great bridge, in the grand market place, is the statue of that wonderful man Erasmus. It is bigger than the life, clad in a Doctor's gown and holding a book in his hand. He was born in 1467 and died at Friburgh in Alsace in the year 1536.[57]

Near to the market-place is the great church of St Laurence. From the tower I had as extensive a view as my eye could command, there being neither hill nor wood to intercept my sight. I saw Delft and the Hague to the north; Dort to the south; Brill to the west; Amsterdam to the east and Utrecht lies off to the south-east.[58]

There are four churches in Rotterdam of the established religion, which is Calvinist, and twelve clergymen to attend them whose stipends are one hundred and seventy pounds per annum each, which is paid out of the revenues of the city. St Laurence is like all other Dutch churches, divested of ornament, gloomy and dark by reason of the numberless atchievements which are hung everywhere round the walls and which are, in general, of black velvet with the arms blazoned, encompassed in a heavy black frame.[59] The naves of the churches are filled with common, rush-bottomed chairs and the isles with little, square wooden boxes into which, in the cold season, are put little stoves and then they quit the isles for more agreeable quarters under the petticoats of the ladies. The altar of this church is divided from the nave by a brass balustrade and heavy pillars of marble.

Among many epitaphs, there was one curious enough to be taken down in writing:

Invicti Herois

Johannis a Brakell

Praetoris, ut dicunt nocturni

Manib: ac. Mem. Sacrum

Hoc tegitur Saxo, Brakelius Œquoris

Horror

Cui Flamma, et Ferrum. cessit et

Unda Maris

Fallimur, an Flammas nunc vomit,

adspice jam, jam

Ferrea qui rupit Vincula, rumpit

Humum[60]

I look on the Exchange, which was finished in 1736, to be the finest building in Rotterdam. It is a quadrangle of freestone, with a light cloister, is much neater, though nothing like so large as our Royal Exchange.

The Weese-house, for orphan children, is likewise a very handsome edifice of freestone, with twenty windows in front. It maintains three hundred boys and as many girls, who are taught to read, write, work and to be both useful and good members of society. There are two considerable charities in this town; the one for old men, the other for old women; and there is likewise an infirmary.

We last night hired a coach which is fixed at a gilder an hour, to take us to Delfs-Hagen, a little village about an hour's distance. The road was very pleasant, being planted on each side with trees. There was nothing sufficiently curious in the place itself to drag us from Rotterdam but, it being a public fair, we wished to see the humours of a Dutch Wake. Children's toys and women's slippers seemed to make the chief figure, there being little else to be sold.

We followed the sound of a fiddle into a little ale-house and walked upstairs into a room full of peasants and tobacco. Here were four girls jumping about, which they call dancing, and thirty or forty men sitting round with their pipes and tobacco, admiring the activity of the nymphs and rolling out such clouds of smoke that we were soon obliged to withdraw to avoid suffocation. From thence we went to a barn to see a Dutch Tragedy and farce. Two of the actresses were tolerably pretty, but Dutch, even from the mouth of a beauty, would be an antidote to venery. It was late in the evening before we got home, notwithstanding which I have risen very early this morning to write you this circumstantially, the journal of the last three days. We purpose leaving Rotterdam this morning, having seen every thing said to be worthy our attention. I am called to breakfast, can therefore only add that we are at the Swine's Hoof, which is well situated, being in the middle of the Market-place. This house is much frequented by the English: a good ordinary both for dinner and supper, where we have met with very genteel people. I should recommend you, by all means, to this inn.

I am, Dear Sir,

Most sincerely yours

Letter IV

Sunday Evening, Aug. 6
Secretary Fagel's Summer House
near the Hague

Dear Sir,

I have found leisure where I least expected it, and pen, ink and paper in a place where I have taken refuge from a storm. I am this moment writing in a summer-house in the centre of the gardens of Griffier Fagel, who is secretary of state.[61]

The fineness of the evening induced us to walk to these gardens, which are only a mile from the Hague; but a thunder storm has suddenly broken over us and forced me to fly to shelter to this place, at the end of the avenue. Where my friends are I know not but hope in as comfortable a situation. Instead of a Dido I have a Dutch gardener with me who can speak only his own language, of which I understand not a single word.[62] I therefore must have recourse to my pen for amusement and, as the storm promises to continue, may probably have time to finish my letter. I confess these gardens are as magnificent as the Dutch gardens can be, where art has left sight of nature. Here is water in abundance, trees out of number and a great extent of ground; but the water consists of stagnated canals, the trees are planted by a line and tortured into form and the extent answers no other purpose than to multiply the dull uniformity.

> *Grove nods at grove, each alley has a brother,*
> *And half the platform just reflects the other.*[63]

I see many buildings dispersed over the gardens in well-chosen spots, especially a temple on a sand hill, which commands the little village of Scheveling, the Hague and the sea. The house is a mere nothing; indeed it is intended only as a little box for retirement from the fatigues of office and bustle of the town.

We left Rotterdam on Thursday morning, returned to Delft in the treckschuyte; walked through the town to the Hague-gate, where we found the boat just ready to push off. The canal from thence to Ryswick is skirted with rows of elms. Instead of going on to the Hague, we got out at the bridge and walked down to the village at almost half a mile's distance. The palace is old, unrepaired and unfurnished, famous only for the peace made there, so advantageous to the Dutch, by the confederate powers of Europe with Lewis XIV in 1697.[64] The prince now and then comes there for half an hour and amuses himself with coursing hares in the courtyard, which is within a wall about fifty yards square. A very princely recreation![65]

We dined at the Strack-huis and met with a comfortable repast which we little expected in such a place. Opposite to the inn lives a Mr Heywood, an Englishman, who is sadler to the Prince; a civil, communicative and, to strangers, an useful man. In the cool of the evening we walked to the Hague, at the distance of two short miles under the shade of a row of elms.

The Hague, in French la Haye, the hedge (the Dutch call it s'Gravenhage, or the Earl's Grove, alluding to a wood which formerly grew there, where the Earls of Holland had a country house) is only a village, not being walled, nor sending deputies to the States. Nevertheless it is residence of all the Foreign Ambassadors, the Seat of Government and, without dispute, the most beautiful place upon earth. On the south lies Delft, on the north the house in the wood, Scheveling and the sea to the west and the great canal of Leyden on the east.

Monday Morning

I was interrupted last night in the middle of my letter by Mr Fagel himself, who on hearing from one of his servants that a stranger had taken shelter in his gardens, as soon as the storm was abated, waited on me and invited me to take the refreshments his house afforded. I found my friends already housed and, after sitting some little time, we made our obeisance and returned to the Hague. I believe I may now proceed without fear of interruption, in giving you an account of this charming place. It is totally surrounded with a canal, over which are many bridges, and a row of lofty trees borders the canal. The streets are so spacious and so much adorned with trees and water that you can scarce conceive yourself in a town; and there are so many squares and public places laid out in shady walks and surrounded with such magnificent buildings that it beggars all description.

I will mention two or three of the most striking parts of the Hague. Among them I think the Vyvetburg has the pre-eminence: it is a kind of square, consisting of several shady walks; on one side a row of magnificent houses, on the other the Vyver, which is a large bason of water faced with stone, two hundred yards in length and near one hundred in breadth; in the center of it is an island planted with trees. One end of the Vyvetburgh opens to the Voorhout which is a large plantation of trees in the middle of which is the Mall, railed on both sides; it is strewed with shells, as are all the walks in Holland, there being neither stone nor gravel in the whole country, the walks are, consequently, unpleasant as the shells never bind but crumble into dust and feel like loose sand under your feet. At the upper end of the Mall is the Hotel of Opdam belonging to Count Wassaner; but the most elegant building in the Hague is the New House (which describes a semi-circle) of the prince of Yeelburgh, who is married to the Prince of Orange's sister.

The New Princess Graft is a row of palaces, rather than of houses, which front the Wood, from which they are divided by a broad canal. Casuari Street is adjoining, in which stands the French Playhouse, a neat little theatre. We were at the Comedy on Friday evening. The actors were tolerably good; Mademoiselle La Roi excellent; Belcour, the celebrated comic actor, to whom the French king has given a pension of two thousand livres, was there but did not act.

I must not omit mentioning to you the prince graft which is half a mile in length, proportionately broad and perfectly straight, with a canal shaded with trees running through the midst of it, over which are thrown many fine stone bridges with iron rails on them.

One of the greatest curiosities in the Hague is the Prince's Cabinet, which is open at twelve o'clock on Fridays and accessible to all strangers who previously send their names. This house was purchased of the Countess of Albemarle, faces the Vyver and is situated on the corner of the outer Court where the horse-guards parade.

In the first room you see a small but excellent collection of Chinese swords, knives and other instruments in gold, richly inlaid with precious stones, and ear-rings, bracelets and such female ornament and apparel. In the next apartment is a good collection of shells, among which the Concha Veneris did not escape my notice being entirely analogous to the name.

In the third room is a brilliant show of precious stones, fossils, minerals and petrifactions. The fourth apartment is filled with various kinds of serpents and small animals, and the last room is ornamented with a large collection of birds extremely well preserved. The Pelican I looked on as the most extraordinary. It is not unlike a stork but has a bill much larger; to the lower part of which hangs a bag of yellow colour that will contain at least a pint.

The distribution and neatness of the whole is admirable and well worthy a stranger's attention.

Very near to the prince's Cabinet is the Prison where the De Witts (the best citizens the Republick knew) died martyrs to the fury and folly of the rabble.[66] It is singular enough to reflect that the vulgar, who were so bigoted to liberty, or rather to licentiousness and anarchy, should on this occasion have deviated so far from those levelling principles as to destroy those real patriots because they opposed the advancement of the prince of Orange (King William III) and wished to preserve their country in its original democratical state.

The palace of the Stadtholder is situated in the center of the town, surrounded by a moat; its external appearance is not very striking, being an old irregular building; but a finer collection of pictures by the Dutch and Flemish masters I have never seen, especially in a little room called the Study, filled by the most capital painters.[67]

The Virgin with the Blessed Infant in her arms—by Raphael.

Adam and Eve in Paradise, surrounded with the birds and beasts—by Rubens.[68]

Portraits—by Rembrandt, Vandyke and Hans Holbein.

A Dutch Kitchen, full of game, fish and flesh, most admirably done—by Teniers.

Many landscapes and fancy pieces—by Gabriel Mutzu,* Jan Steen,+ Potter# and Wouvermans.[69]

---

* Metzu was born at Leyden in 1658, died under the operation of cutting for the stone. His subjects were usually taken from low life; such as women selling fish, fowls or hares; sick persons attended by the doctor; chymists in the laboratories; dead game; painters shops, and drawing rooms hung with prints. He finished with extreme neatness—painted portraits well and approached near to Vandyke. [Gabriel Metsu's dates were, in fact 1629–1667. Ed.]

+ Jan Steen was born at Leyden in 1689, was remarkable for his conversations and drolls. His drawing is sometimes censurable but his design was generally correct, his figures well disposed and his characters strongly marked. [Jan Steen's dates were, in fact, 1625/6–1679. Ed.]

Paul Potter was born at Enkhysen in 1625, he was an expert master at 15. His subjects were landscapes with different animals but principally cows, sheep and goats which he painted in the highest perfection.

I look on this room as complete; there is not a picture but may be dwelt on with delight. In the next room are two courtezans in crayon by Bolomeii; the one has a black veil thrown over the side of her face, the other has a slight cymar over her bosom, but the painter has made it so transparent that he has left but little for the imagination.[70]

Abraham sacrificing Isaac in ivory is inimitably carved.

In the other apartments, among many fine pieces, you will find a very large one by Potter painted in 1647—the design is a peasant looking at his cattle, the flies on the cows seem alive and a toad sitting on the grass has equal excellence.[71]

There are some fruit and game pieces by Weenix,[*] well done; and some excellent pieces on copper by Rothenamer.[+]

Abraham offering up Isaac by Leonardo da Vinci.[72]

Two landscapes by Vernet.[73]

Jeptha's rash vow by Coypel. This is esteemed his masterpiece and applauded by the best judges and was celebrated by the poets of the time.[74]

A Dutch room in which are two women and a child in the cradle which is wonderfully done by Douw.[75] Sixteen hundred ducats were refused for this piece. There is nothing superb in the furniture, nor in the size of the apartments; the pictures are the only thing which are worthy attention.

On the other side of the quadrangle is the chamber of the states where the business of the States-General is transacted.[76] It is hung with green cloth and all the ornaments are the pictures of the princes of Orange. The chamber where the Ambassadors are received is of the same size and looks upon the Vyver. At the upper end of the room is a fine piece of William the third. The carpet under his feet has been much admired. The little room adjoining is the chamber to which the ministers withdraw for private conferences. It is made most valuable by twelve little pieces, giving the history of Claudius Civilis by Hans Holbein, for which the great Lord Bolingbroke offered ten thousand

---

[*] This was John Weenix the son, who was born at Amsterdam in 1644, he far surpassed his father, who was much esteemed. His usual subjects were animals of every kind, landscapes and flowers, with some game pieces. [In fact, often difficult to tell the work of the father Jan Baptist from that of the son Jan, 1642–1719. Ed.]

[+] John Rothenamer was born in Munich in 1564; painted historical subjects on copper, of a very small size, imitated Tintoretto—painted both in fresco and oil. [Johann Rottenhamer, 1564–1625. Ed.]

pounds.[77] This Claudius Civilis was a Batavian of royal descent, as mentioned by Tacitus, who commanded eight cohorts of his countrymen, at that time allies to the Romans, but Vitellius, the Emperor, charged him with treason and he narrowly escaped with his life; hence, his inveterate hatred of the Romans. Under the mask of attachment to Vespasian in the beginning of the wars between him and Vitellius, but in reality to free his countrymen from the Roman yoke, he diverted the young Batavians from enlisting under the ensigns of Vitellius. This occasioned a long war in which Claudius acquitted himself as a consummate General. At length, in the first year of Vespasian, he was obliged to submit to Cerealis, the Roman general; on the one side an entire submission, on the other an unreserved pardon.[78]

On the Saturday evening we entertained ourselves by viewing the house in the wood, a palace belonging to the Prince of Orange, situated about a mile from the Hague, at the extremity of the wood, which is chiefly of oak.[79] This is about a mile in extent but not above half as wide. It is the only wood in Holland, except a small one at the gates of Harlem. The house was built by Amalia, widow of Henry Frederick, the Third Prince of Orange. There is nothing grand in the outward appearance, nor superb in the apartments; it was meant for a place of retirement, not for a palace. The saloon, which is the only good room, is of octagonal form, with a dome painted and a cupola, round which is a gallery for the musick. This apartment is covered with paintings, admirably well done by different hands; but Vulcan's forge, near the chimney, points out the master to be Rubens.[80]

On each side of the saloon are the Prince and Princess's apartments, consisting of a suite of three rooms, bedchamber, dressing room and closet. Round the princess's bed is a rail of Japan, inlaid with mother of pearl, which cost three thousand pounds. The doors of the dressing room are painted with full-length figures; and the Japan closet is wainscotted with Japan, and there are little doors in different parts of it which slide back and shew you some curious Chinese figures, fixed in recesses of six or eight inches square.

The common dining room is full of pictures by the princess Anne, daughter of George II and mother of the present Prince of Orange. They are rather better done than might have been expected from a Princess.[81]

The chimney pieces are of marble, ill-executed and heavy. The garden, even in the Dutch taste, has little or no merit; but the wood is disposed in pretty walks, did not the loose sand make the walking on them intolerable.

Yesterday morning we walked down to Scheveling, a fishing village about two miles from hence. The road is cut through the Sand-hills, which appear to me to be the derelicts of the ocean. The center, for carriages, is nicely paved; the footpath on each side is of sand, covered with sea-shells, which answer the purpose of gravel. A double row of trees screens you totally from the sun and gives a most agreeable gloom. This walk is straight as a line and the steeple of Scheveling closes the avenue.[82] You do not see the sea till you are within a few yards of it when the main ocean opens up to your view. It was singular to me, who have been used to see the beach covered with gravel and racks, to behold here nothing but sand and shells which the sea throws up in incredible quantities. A shower of rain hastened us back again much sooner than we intended and deprived us of the pleasure of seeing the Portland Gardens which join the road but we have taken advantage of the cool of the morning to walk down to these agreeable gardens. They are only half a mile from the gate that leads to Scheveling, to the left of the road. There is a fine Orangerie, in the form of an amphitheatre, the centre of which is a music room. These gardens, or rather pleasure grounds, are very extensive and extremely elegant. Serpentine walks, artificial hill and dale, thickets and many forest trees with seats and statues well disposed, all allure you, that the master is indebted to the English for the superiority he has gained over the miserable taste of his countrymen.[83] His son, Mr Bentinck, is now a captain of an English man-of-war.[84]

There are some Jet-Eaus, which are childish; remnants, I suppose, of Dutch humour. For instance, as you walk over a bridge, nicely paved, by turning a cock a thousand little fountains play up through the interstices of the stones. Again, at the end of one of the walks is a chair from the seat of which springs a fountain the moment you have seated yourself to the refreshment perhaps of your body, in a warm day, but to the utter demolition of your clothes.

The grotto is done in much better taste. The moment you enter it the water flows from the threshold in a number of little streams; and from the far corners of the grotto fountains spring through the rock-work with force sufficient to strike the top, which fall down into large shells in such manner that you doubt whether the water rises from the floor or drops from the ceiling.

As we came back, we looked into the great Church which has nothing remarkable about it but the tomb of Admiral Waassanaars, Baron d'Opdam. His ship was blown up by the English under the command of the Duke of York in 1666.[85] Round the church we saw many storks walking about as tame as our turkies. They are somewhat in shape like a heron. Their colour is white, their wings are tipped with black. They live upon the offal of the fish market which is near the church. I have seen numbers of them in the meadows, though they are esteemed birds of passage and at this season they are not very common. The vulgar error is that these birds are so fond of Liberty that they will only live in a republick. I am sure, in point of policy, they cannot live in a more desirable country as they have fish and frogs in abundance for their food and the utmost security for themselves, it being deemed a crime to maltreat or kill them.

I do not recollect anything more extraordinary. I have sitten till I am recovered indeed from the fatigue of my morning's walk but am most horribly tired with writing. I am summoned to dinner—shall go to Leyden in the evening.

Adieu!

Hague
Monday Noon
7th August

Letter V

Dear Sir

On Monday evening we went in the treckschuyte to Leyden with a Dutch General we had lived with at the Table d'Hote at the Hague. The distance was ten miles but the whole canal being lined with summer houses and pleasure gardens belonging to the inhabitants of those towns, who in the summer retire to these little boxes, made the scene appear most beautiful and the distance nothing.

When we arrived at the inn we were recommended to we found it filled by the French Ambassador and his train and, for want of an interpreter, we wandered about the town till it was very dark and met with two or three disagreeable circumstances which made me lament my ignorance of the Dutch language; but at length we found the Golden Ball, an English house, and with my wants vanished my desire of talking Dutch.

Leyden is esteemed, in point of size, the second city in Holland but its trade is now inconsiderable which in the woollen manufactory was formerly very extensive.

This city is surrounded with a rampart and a very wide canal. The Esplanade and the Fosse are adorned with rows of trees which environ the town with a pleasant walk at the water's edge from whence you look over some rich meadows. In the centre of the town is a Tumulus of considerable height, surrounded by a brick wall from whence you have a tolerable view of the city. It is called the Berg or Hengist's Castle, was built by Hengist the Saxon, as a trophy for his conquest of England.

The most elegant street is the Broad Street which runs from the Hague gate to the Utrecht gate: it is a little on the curve which adds, I think, much to its beauty. The pavement is extremely fine and the street rises in the centre, like the new-paved streets of London; is very spacious as indeed are most of the streets in Leyden. Among the canals the Rapinburg is the most beautiful; the houses are magnificent, the bridges stone with iron rails and there are trees on either side of the canal.[86] It is said that there are an hundred and forty-five bridges and an hundred and eighty streets within the city of Leyden. The Old Rhine runs through this town and loses itself in the little village of Catwick which lies in the neighbourhood.

The University is the most renowned of the five* which are in the United Provinces and is the most ancient being founded in 1575, by the states, as a reward to the inhabitants for defending themselves against the Spaniards during a six month's siege, in which they suffered all the horrors and extremities of famine.

The Academy abounds with many curiosities. It is there the professors read lectures to the students who lodge in the town and are not distinguished by any academical habit.[87] It is here that the learned Scaliger, Leipsius, Salmasius and Boerhaave gained so much reputation by their lectures and brought students from all parts of Europe to attend them.[88]

The Physick Garden, for ought I know, may be curious; but as I scarce know an Aloe from a Sensitive Plant, I cannot pretend to determine.[89] There seemed to be a very great variety, nicely arranged and taken care of. I saw two little trees in pots, the one was the green the other the bohea tea; the first has a sharp, narrow leaf, the other is much larger and is round towards the end.

The coffee tree grows from a simple leader, exactly like the branch of a vine; the leaf is not very unlike the leaf of the orange tree, to which the flower bears some resemblance.

On one side of these gardens is a very curious collection of antique marbles given by Gerard Papenbrochius, a Burgomaster of Amsterdam.[90] I cannot omit mentioning the statues of Hercules, and of Bacchus leaning on a fawn and attended by a tyger, of Abundantia as big as life, and of a naked Apollo; all of which have especial merit.

Adjoining to the statues is the Natural Philosophy School in which the lectures are read. You will find in it a good collection of natural curiosities;

		A.D.
*	The five universities are	
	Leyden in Holland	1575
	Utrecht " "	1636
	Franeker in Friesland	1584
	Groningen " "	1614
	Harderwick in Gelderland	1648

[Franeker University flourished from 1585–1811; Harderwijk closed in the same year. Ed.]

some very fine petrefactions, in particular a piece of oak, one side of which has been polished and vies, both in hardness and colour, with an agate. Some curious pieces of crystal, formed by nature to an apex with six angles, as exact and as finely polished as if the production of art. A fish, called the medusa's head, from a thousand little fibres darting out from its body in a circle like twisted rays. This itself is sufficiently curious but the exact representation of it, in a natural agate, is much more so.

But I think one of the greatest curiosities was the asbestos from Transylvania. It is a stone with a soft down on it, like velvet of a dove colour. Of this is made both paper and linen—we saw samples of both. The very peculiar property of it is that the fire has no effect on it, for it still continues its form unchanged and unconsumed.

Among the beasts was an ermin, about the size and shape of a weasel. This little animal is so fearful of dirtying its skin that it will sooner lose its liberty than its cleanliness.

There was a kind of toad that brings forth its young from its back. On observing it, we perceived infinite numbers of young toads adhering to the back which appeared like the broken scales of a fish.

The toad fish from America is an extraordinary creature. It is for the first six months a toad, then changes by degrees into a fish. This had half completed its transformation, having the tail of a fish with the head and foreparts of a toad.

The Penna Marina belongs to the animal species. It is the production of the ocean; looks like a plant and is nothing more than a stem of about two inches long with a kind of feather at the end of it, not unlike a quill, with part of the feather cut off.

Among the feathered race the most curious was the Hydrocorax Indicus; the only one in Europe; larger than a turkey, black, Rostro unicorni, cornu recurvo, if I may express myself in the technical terms of Ornithology. The casuari is likewise black and, in size, equal to an ostrich.

There was an immense beast called the Hypopotamus, as large as an elephant, its colour black, with a row of grinders in the interior part of its mouth, besides a good number in front.

From the Academy you cross the Rapinbury to the public library.[91] There are some valuable portraits of their literati; in particular an original of Erasmus by Hans Holbein. They have done us the honour to give place in their library to the Sçavans Anglois in busts of ivory.

I was a little surprised to see, among my learned countrymen, Marvel and Ludlow; none but Dutchmen could have introduced them to the company of Lock and Milton.[92] There are vast piles of civil law and a considerable number of manuscripts but, these excepted, it can be called but an indifferent collection. Near to the library is the Anatomy School in which are many curiosities: some Roman antiques such as Urna feralis in red potter's clay, the same as our earthenware utensils; a Lucerna Sepulchralis, which was the perpetual lamp used by the Romans; it is made with four spouts and rises up in the middle in a conical form.

There was the egg of a crocodile which is of a brown colour and of a hard substance, the inside looked like cedar wood.

From the Anatomy School we went to the Stadt-house which is situated in the Broad Street and has a long front in the true Dutch style of architecture. The famous picture of the day of Judgement by Luke of Leyden* is preserved in one of the chambers of the Stadt-house.[93] It is painted on wood, in three compartments which, by the help of hinges, fold together and protect the piece.

In the grand Compartment you see our Saviour enthroned on the center of a rainbow, the extremities of which lose themselves imperceptibly in the clouds. The twelve elders are seated on each side; below there is a group of mortals who have not received judgement which you may easily discern by the suspense and anxiety so strongly impressed on their countenances. On one side of this group you see those who have received the reward of their virtue, escorted by the good angels who are flying into the heavens with the just. On the other side are some of the oddest looking devils that the most luxuriant imagination can conceive; especially one with the head of a cow and with two long meager dugs hanging down to the middle—it is impossible to behold this fiend without horror. These are employed in dragging away the condemned by the hair of the head and pushing them forward with pitch-forks. I am concerned for the ladies but I could not help observing among those who were howling and gnashing their teeth, a vast majority of female

---

* Lucius van Leyden died in 1533, aged 39; he painted not only in oil but in distemper and on glass and was full as eminent for engraving as for painting. His genius exerted itself so early that, before he was 15, he painted the history of St Hubert which procured him the greatest applause. His tone of colouring is good, his attitudes (allowing for the stiff German taste) are well enough, his figures have a considerable expression and his pictures are highly finished. He endeavoured to proportion the strength of his colouring to the different degrees of distance in which his objects were placed, for in that age the true principles of perspective were but little known. As he had no instruction in this branch he was consequently incorrect with regard to the proportional height of his figures to their distances, so as to appear a mannerist.

figures, with golden tresses flowing down their backs, some of whom had not so far forgotten their humanity but that they attempted to impose even on the devils, by eluding their grasp and running backwards towards the mansions of the blessed.

In the next apartment is a crucifixion by the same hand. Here you see our Saviour on the cross, the two thieves on each side and a thousand distinct figures in which the passions are finely varied. Prostrate at the foot of the cross were vast numbers of the fair sex in all the pageantry of woe, with their hair dishevelled and their eyes streaming with tears, but I doubt that they were crocodile's tears or I should not have seen such numbers guarded by devils in the other picture.

In this room is a fine piece by Moor of the first Brutus seeing his judgement executed on his sons; one of which lies a lifeless trunk, the head rolling in the dust, the other son is on his knees expecting the fatal stroke.[94] There is, likewise, a tolerable picture of the well-known story of Scipio and the Celtiberian captive and a large picture which describes the people of Leyden, after being relieved from the Spaniards and the famine, devouring with well-executed eagerness the long awaited food.[95]

As Leyden consists chiefly of people in trade, which is at present greatly on the decline, you may suppose the town to be what in fact it was, extremely dull; we therefore left it on Wednesday morning and proceeded on the canal to Harlem.

The Veens, or Turf-Pits, may be seen from thence, of which the greatest part appear to be full of water and little likely to be productive of fuel; notwithstanding four hundred thousand people who inhabit the three neighbouring cities are supplied from them.

This was but a dull voyage, the Sand-hills lying on the left and Harlem-meer on the right which is a lake almost fourteen miles in length and of equal breadth. It lies between Leyden and Harlem and Amsterdam, is navigable* but subject to storms and some melancholy accidents have happened on it, which occasioned the canals to be made from Leyden to Amsterdam, a much longer passage but the safety of it induces most travellers to prefer the more tedious method, especially as you then pass through Harlem which is a large city containing, agreeable to the computation made in 1732, between forty

---

* The king of Bohemia having been dethroned and driven out of the Palatinate by the Emperor, took sanctuary in Holland. In November 1629, as he was passing over the lake, the evening came on and the weather tempestuous, when a boat ran foul of his and immediately sank it. The King saved his life by swimming but his eldest son was drowned.

and fifty thousand inhabitants. It differs so little from the other towns I have seen that I need only mention the church which is the largest in Holland and adorned with an organ which is infinitely superior to anything of the kind in Europe.* It was made by Christian Mullar of Harlem and erected in 1738. It consists of eight thousand pipes, the largest one thirty-eight feet long and fifteen inches in diameter. There are sixty-eight stops of which the most wonderful is the Vox humana, so exactly imitative of the human voice, both in the base, tenor and treble, that it was some time before I could persuade myself I was not imposed on by real voices. There were other pipes which were equally wonderful in the notes of different birds and the kettledrum stop was beyond all imagination.[96]

Opposite this church lives a bookseller who, very civilly, showed us the first, second and third attempts of Laurence Costar, the inventor of printing. The first is on a narrow leaf of parchment in duodecimo. The second attempt was on paper in octavo. The third, likewise is on paper, in quarto, in which he brought it to a tolerable degree of perfection. It is printed only on one side, with a print at top from a wooden impression, of equal merit with those which ornament our English ballads.[97]

Laurence Costar was an Alderman of Harlem and in 1440 it is said he hit upon this invention, as he was walking in the wood near Harlem, by cutting the bark of beech trees into letters and then stamping them upon paper, as a seal.[+98] He soon changed these for leaden letters and these afterwards into pewter; but while he was at church with his family, John Faust, his servant, stole the printing materials and carried them to Mentz, where he pretended that he had invented the art, from whence he acquired the title Dr Faustus, the conjuror of Mentz.[99] The most useful improvement in this art was made by John Mentel who discovered the method of casting letters. Aldus Minutius, the famous Venetian printer, soon after found out the italic characters and was the first to print in Greek and Hebrew.[100]

In the street adjacent to the other end of the church is a house belonging, I believe, to the city in which are some few good pictures which formerly

---

*   It plays on Tuesdays and Thursdays from noon till one o'clock. At other times you must give a ducat to the organist and half a crown to the blower of the bellows.

+   Philip, Peter and John Wouvermans were born at this place: the two latter copied the manner and were far inferior to Philip who was infinitely beyond all his contemporaries. His chief subjects were huntings, hawkings, encampments of armies, farriers shops and all kind of scenes which afforded him a proper opportunity of introducing horses, which he painted to the greatest perfection.

hung in the palace of Count Florence the fifth; especially three by Cornelius of Harlem: Herod killing the Innocents; the feast of the gods, in which the sole of Vulcan's foot will strike you; the other is a Friar and Nun but much damaged by the damp.[101]

There is an excellent piece of a Dutch Girl in the style of a peasant, with an archness in her look that never Dutch woman, I believe, was blessed with.[102]

The Spaniards, commanded by the son of the Duke of Alva, besieged this place in 1573; which being reduced to the greatest extremities, after a desperate defence for ten months, was forced to surrender and two thousand of the inhabitants were basely murdered, contrary to the terms of the capitulation.[103]

The trade of Harlem consists chiefly in bleaching of linen. The holland and cambrick made in Flanders and great quantities of Irish linen are sent there to be whitened; the slimy water of the Meer being acknowledged superior to any waters upon earth for bleacheries. They have likewise considerable manufactories in velvet and silk which they vend chiefly at Leipsick and Hamburg. We only stayed to dine at Harlem, in the evening proceeded in the treckshuyte to Amsterdam. About mid-day we were obliged to change boats and pass over the sluices which are of enormous size. On the right lies Harlem Meer, the river Y washes the left. It is five miles from this place to Amsterdam and the canal that whole distance is as straight as a line but the banks are not built on as the canals from Rotterdam to the Hague and Leyden, which is owing to want of room, the lake and the river being too near.

It is curious to observe the water of the Y four or five feet higher than the adjacent country; but, in fact, almost every canal has the water raised above the adjacent meadows. When we landed at Amsterdam we found common fame to be no lyar [sic] in respect of the insufferable stench arising from the canals and common shores.

Amsterdam is situated on the river Amstel* and an arm of the sea called the Y, at the mouth of the Zuyder-sea, and is built in the form of a crescent. It is fortified with a fosse of great depth and width; with a rampart of earth faced with brick, strengthened with twenty-six bastions, in each of which stands a wind-mill, ornamented with eight magnificent gates of free-stone,

---

* Over the Amstel, which enters at the Utrecht gate, is thrown a bridge of eleven arches, eight of which are shut to enclose the yachts belonging to the city. This bridge is much admired by the natives; in my opinion it is a very paltry piece of Architecture, the arches being very high and narrow.

built either in a semi-circular or octagonal shape. In all the chief streets there are canals shaded with trees, the grandest of which is the Heere-graft, or canal of Lords. This is the place of residence for the bankers and chief merchants; for here everyone is in trade, the few nobles of Holland reside always at the Hague. Those streets in which there are no canals are vilely narrow. The Ness, in which we live, I had the curiosity to measure and it is only sixteen feet wide: the houses are lofty and the bridges are chiefly of stone.

The squares are neither spacious nor elegant. The Dam is the largest in which the Stadthouse is situated but it is irregular and vilely disfigured by a weighing house.[104] The others no more deserve the name of square than Clare Market or Palace Yard, Westminster.

This populous city contained twenty-six thousand and thirty-five houses in 1732 and is supposed, according to the best calculation, to contain at present two hundred and fifty thousand inhabitants,* was at the beginning of the thirteenth century an inconsiderable fishing village on the edge of a morass which is now covered with buildings erected upon piles of timber driven into the earth at immense labour and expence. For the foundations only of one tower six thousand trees were rammed into the ground. Notwithstanding these precautions, the magistrates are so apprehensive of the foundations that very few coaches are licensed. The carriages in general are fixed on sledges drawn by one horse, the driver attending on foot.

There are fifteen churches of the established, that is the Calvinist, religion which are served by thirty ministers, equal in authority and revenue. They are allowed two hundred and forty pounds per year each, which is paid by the city.

The most stupendous undertaking in this city is the Stadthouse which you enter by seven small gates, parallel to each other, instead of one magnificent portal, equal to a front which extends itself two hundred and eighty-two feet, whose height is one hundred and sixteen and the breadth two hundred and thirty-two feet. This building is of stone, with pillars of the Corinthian order. It is erected on thirteen thousand six hundred and fifty-nine piles of timber, and was finished in 1655. On the top is a statue of Atlas in brass bearing on his shoulders a copper globe, said to be larger than that at St Peter's in Rome;

---

* Paris is said to contain five hundred thousand and London seven hundred thousand inhabitants. The number of inhabitants in Holland are twelve hundred thousand; in England are computed to be nine million, in France eighteen million and in Germany twenty millions of souls.

and on the center is a cupola from whence is an extensive view of the city and its environs. The piles cost one hundred thousand—the whole expence was computed at two millions. Versailles cost only eight hundred thousand pounds, the Escurial one million and St Paul's one million five hundred thousand pounds. "It is on record that St Peter's at Rome with all that is contained in it has cost near thirteen million sterling."

The cornices of the rooms are finely carved, the floor laid with marble and the sides of the apartment lined either with marble or valuable paintings. Over the doors and chimney pieces are several historical pieces in *basso relievo* inimitably executed in Italian marble; and there are some deceptions in a kind of grey painting, to imitate *basso relievo,* (especially of some children) by De Wit, so finely touched that the most critical eye at half the distance of the room would be deceived.[105]

A large piece by Vandyke is deservedly esteemed. It is a feast given to the Spanish Ambassador by the Burgomasters of Amsterdam on the making peace between the two countries. An old grey-haired man is so much admired in this wonderful picture that seven thousand gilders were offered to cut out the head. But the best piece is by Vanderhelst in 1648 which represents an entertainment where you see the portraits of all the considerable persons of the city.[106]

The Stadthouse is admirably contrived to public utility. Here is the bank, supposed to be the richest in Europe; here are the courts of justice, the prisons for criminals and debtors; the chambers of the senate, the treasury, the magazine of arms and, in short, all the public offices; with eight large cisterns of water on the top, with pipes to every room to extinguish fires. The citizens hall is the grandest being one hundred and twenty feet by fifty seven and ninety feet high. It is paved with marble, in which are stained the terrestrial and celestial globes; the sides, the roof and the pillars are all of marble but there always is a something wanting—there is not light enough to admire with nicety the wonderful magnificence of this apartment.

From the Stadthouse you cross the Dam to the Exchange, which is not to be compared with Rotterdam in beauty nor to our Royal Exchange in size. The building is of brick and at full Change, if appearances are to be relied on, was crowded with the most blackguard fellows on the face of the earth. In the afternoon I paid a second visit to the Exchange to see the city militia perform their exercise; to which every man is subject unless he makes a pecuniary compensation; those therefore who from their poverty cannot, or from their avarice will not pay the fine, are obliged to serve. Here penury and parsimony were collected together in such various habits (for they have no regular uniform) as to make the most ludicrous group imagination can suggest. A giant and a dwarf, a Falstaff and a slender, a bob wig and a shock head of hair; in coats of all the colours of the rainbow, joined most heterogeneously together to compose a rank, in which every man followed his own inventions, in as many different attitudes and manoeuvres as there were men to make them.

In the evening we went to the theatre, which, like all playhouses, our own excepted, is dark, long and small. The pit is excellent, having seats with low backs and marked with numbers to distinguish the seat of each person, by which both crowding and disputes are prevented. This is the only house I ever saw abroad in which there are seats in the pit, or *parterre,* as it is called. It is under the control and direction of the city; the magistrates receive the money, defray the charges and pay the actors; the residue is applied to the maintenance of the poor and to support the different hospitals. Every rope dancer, puppet player, as well as others who pretend to entertain the publick are obliged to contribute one third of their profits towards the maintenance of the poor.

On Friday we looked into the Rasphouse which is a prison for criminals as well as for children who are profligate or disobedient: the former are confined to a small room, chained to a block and spend their whole time sawing or *rasping* Brazil wood, or in some other work equally laborious.[107] I was shocked at the sight of so many of my species, naked to the waist, worn out with labour, pale with confinement and emaciated by want. How much wiser this method than the English law which for thirteen pence deprives a man of his life and the king of a subject whom, the Dutch show us, may be made useful to the publick.

From thence we went to the Spinhouse, for the correction but not I think to the amendment of loose women, as every one is permitted to see and converse with them through the rails which can only harden them in impudence.[108]

We walked into the New Church to see a burial: in this nation of industry time is too precious to be complimented away on the dead, who can make them no return; therefore the ceremony of prayers is laid aside as superfluous. The coffin is put instantly into the grave, which is immediately filled up; the relations bow and return to their avocations. The organ in this church is inferior only to the organ at Harlem. The partition which divides the chancel from the nave is of Corinthian brass. The sounding board over the pulpit is justly admired for the inimitable carving with which it is ornamented.

From thence we proceeded to the Admiralty and Dock-Yard, which are situated at the extremity of the quay. The Admiralty forms three sides of a square, the middle of which is the yard for the building of men of war; the forth side is open to the water. Here is not an appearance to be feared by the English, tho' much to be admired for the excellent order in which the arms stored are disposed.

Among the number of hospitals in this city the Gast-house for the sick is the most worthy of a stranger's visiting. It is an elegant stone quadrangle, at the end of which are some neat little shops for toys, lace etc. The revenue of this hospital is computed at eight hundred pounds sterling a year, a large sum but the general hospital for men at Madrid contains one thousand five hundred iron beds and its revenue amounts to forty thousand doubloons, about thirty thousand pounds sterling.

There is a hospital where all poor travellers without distinction are lodged and entertained for three nights and no longer. It is computed that twenty thousand souls are maintained in the different hospitals; which are either endowed or supported out of the public revenue; assisted by the contributions of the charitable, for which purpose men belonging to the hospitals go twice a week to every house begging for alms.

After supper we amused ourselves at a Musico, which is a licensed brothel. You enter a large room upon the payment of a gilder, for which you have wine, musick and tobacco. There you see girls of all sorts and nations who do not live in the house, neither are any flagrant indecencies permitted. If you chuse to retire with a lady to her lodgings there is no law to restrain or punish you. It is as morally evil to license fornication as it is politically so to shut up for life women who have shewn themselves willing to become fruitful members of society.

We found the women equally ugly, impudent and disgusting; we soon therefore retired unhurt by the smiles of the Harlots or the snick and snees of the Sailors which they are very ready with if a man is unfortunate enough to pitch upon a girl who is the favourite of one of these savages.[109]

This morning (Saturday) we went to the Portuguese synagogue which is a large spacious building, filled with a numerous congregation. The women sit together in a gallery, with lattices before them. The men sit below on benches with Tawlises* on, which they throw over their shoulders and, I declare, I took the assembly for old clothes men with their bags over their arms.[110]

---

* The *Tawlis* is a kind of vail, generally thrown over the shoulders, sometimes over the face.

From thence we hurried down to the Quay where we had a vessel ready for us and sailed with a fair wind over the Zuyder Zee to Sardam,* a village in North Holland famous for ship-building and wind-mills, which latter seem to be innumerable.[111] Had Don Quixote in his travels touched at Sardam he would have found there adventures for life without searching for other conquests. The first mill we visited was a saw mill, by which forty boards can be sawed at the same time. The flies of the mill are fixed to a large beam which turns on an axle. In the center of this beam is the grand wheel which puts in motion another immediately below it. This is likewise fixed on the middle of a piece of timber, which hangs on an axle and to which four perpendicular saws, ten in each compartment, are fixed; which, as the wheel goes round, are elevated and again thrust down. At the end of this beam are two iron hooks which catch a wheel and each time the saws go up and down, it moves the wheel one cog, that wheel moves another which catches into a piece of this iron and draws it towards itself. At the end of this iron is a cross bar, which presses against the end of the tree, while the other end is sawing and pushes it on to the teeth of the saw, with a motion proportionate to the dispatch of the saws.

From the saw mill we walked to a paper mill and observed the whole process from the cutting rags to the cleaning them in a wheel with a constant succession of fresh water which makes it into a pulp. A mould, with wire at top and bottom, is dipped in. On taking it out the wire top slips off, a piece of flannel is laid on the paper which the next moment is portable and hung out to dry, the flaws being picked out which is the business of the women and children. The last process is to press it.

From thence we passed to a tobacco mill, in which is a large trough full of leaf. Ten or twelve perpendicular pieces of timber with choppers fixed to one end and cogs to the other which catch in wheel as it turns, by which they are lifted up, fall by their own weight and chop the tobacco small. It is then laid out on a stone table on which move two immense stones, one within the other. The first spreads it, a machine of wood follows and collects it into a row, which a piece of iron comes after and divides into a furrow wide enough for the pressure of the other stone. All these move at the same time and turn on the same axle.

The oil mill for turnip seed &c. is on the same principles, to bruise them into powder, which is then put into a pan over the fire for a moment, from thence into

---

*   In the church is a picture remarkable not for the goodness of the painting but for the extraor-
     dinary fact it is intended to perpetuate. A woman was tossed by a bull when big with child
     and gored in the belly with his horn; the moment she fell to the ground she was delivered of a
     son—they both survived, as did the husband who was tossed in coming to her assistance.

little bags, two of which are put into a press, one at each end, which are pressed by a wedge in the middle and force the water into vases below. The bags are then slipped off, the dust remains a hard cake, with which they feed the cattle.

From Sardam we sailed back to Buiksloot, a little village in North Holland, opposite to Amsterdam. A droll custom is retained in North Holland of having a door in every house which is never opened but when a corpse is carried out, which must be brought thro' that door and no other. The head-dress of the women is very extraordinary. There is a little hair cut very short and thin which is combed down on the forehead and powdered. The cap sticks close to their ears, under which are two little pieces of silver or gold which appear at each temple and a large piece, like a broad ribbon, is under the cap on the back part of the head.

There we took a waggon to Broek about six miles distance, the most picturesque village perhaps in the world.[112] It is chiefly inhabited by bankers and insurers. The houses are of fluted boards painted in different colours agreeable to the taste of the respective owners. The roofs are of glazed tiles and the gardens, which are before every door, are laid out in parterres of various forms and colours by the assistance of shells, marbles, glass beads &c. A few trees are planted before every house at the extremity of these little gardens, which are cut into form.

The streets are paved with brick on which neither carriages nor cattle are suffered and they are as clean as a lady's drawing room. Nothing can be conceived neater than that beautiful little place, nor more extravagant than the charges at the inn. Some boiled perch and three bottles of Rhenish, which is about ten-pence a bottle, cost us a Guinea. We returned to Buiksloot to our vessel and, as the wind slackened we narrowly escaped lying out all night in a boat without a cabin, for towards the side of the harbour the city is enclosed with great piles driven into the ground joined by large beams placed horizontally with openings to let the vessels in and out which is done without the least confusion. These openings are shut every evening at the ringing of the bell and we were so near being too late as to touch the beam with the side of our boat as it was closing the harbour. I am fatigued with the excursion I have made, I have written till my candles are almost out, as well as my eyes; I must rise early, as we go to Utrecht in the morning, therefore I must bid you

Adieu!

Midnight, Saturday
12 August

Amsterdam

Letter VI

Dear Sir,

I left Amsterdam at seven this morning and have for the first time found a Treckschuyte disagreeable; but as it is probably the last that I shall ever meet with, a few unpleasant hours must not be regarded.

We unluckily could not get the roof and as it rains hard we cannot walk upon the top; we therefore have no alternative than to fit in the body of the Boat with upwards of twenty persons of both sexes from whose mouths nothing has hitherto issued but volumes of Tobacco smoke, which has made my friends sick and me sulky. I wish to beguile the time by writing but I gave you so long an account of Amsterdam last night that I have nothing more to add. Observations you cannot expect from a man whose furlough is so short that he is obliged to go post thro' the country. Such an excursion, however pleasing to the eye, cannot give much improvement to the mind. In little more than a fortnight I have made the tour of the whole province of Holland, visited every town (except Dort and Tergow which, on inquiry, I find not worthy notice) and have suffered nothing curious to escape me.[114] My head therefore is a confused medly of dykes and pictures, churches and canals, bridges and stadthouses, but a void in respect to the customs, police and manners of the people, the only useful knowledge to be acquired by travelling.[115]

I have seen enough to confirm me in the justness of Sir William Temple's opinion, who in speaking of Holland, if my memory misleads me not, says "that it is a country where the earth is better than the air, and profit more in request than honour; where there is more sense than wit, more good-nature than good-humour, and more wealth than pleasure. Where a man would chuse rather to travel than to live; shall find more things to observe than desire; and more persons to esteem than to love".[116]

There are regulations in the police of Amsterdam, which will be well worthy of imitation in London. You never meet a Watchman alone, two always walk together, by which means they add strength as well as give courage to each other. Many a house is broken open in London and many a sober citizen knocked down in presence of a watchman, who either from fear or knavery, suffers the villains to escape. There is another admirable custom to prevent the spreading of Fire by giving an almost immediate alarm. On the top of four churches situated at four different quarters of the city, watchmen are fixed for the whole night who are obliged to sound a trumpet every half hour as a signal of their being awake and on their duty. On the breaking out of fire the alarm bell is rung, the watchmen are collected and are at the spot in a moment. Of what infinite service would a plan something similar to this be in our metropolis!

There are few general conveniences which carry not a mischief along with them; canals, for instance, are great ornaments to the streets and of infinite use to the Inhabitants but the mischief is that many an honest man loses his life in Amsterdam who in London would only lose his memory; for the villains first rob him and then push him into the canal to prevent his telling tales; thus charitably easing him of his money lest the weight of it should sink him.

I believe I have already mentioned the neatness of the people; but in this they have no merit, for the neatness of their houses and the cleanliness of their towns proceed from necessity; such is the moisture of the air that, were it not for these customs, pestilential diseases would be the consequence which, careful as they are, now often happen. This perpetual dampness in the atmosphere rusts metals and moulds wood, which obliges the Inhabitants, not from a principle of neatness but of œconomy, by scouring the one and painting the other, to seek a prevention or a cure. Hence arises that neatness which by people who judge only from appearances is called *natural*; but indeed most national customs are the effects of unobserved causes or necessities. In this country the mind is perpetually struck with wonder and admiration; if Mathematicians are to be credited, on the measure of the two elements, they found the sea, even in a calm, above half a foot higher than the land; the waves are checked by an infinity of sand hills, which lie along the coast. Add to this natural defense a Dyke of twenty feet high, twenty-five feet broad at bottom and about ten at top, running parallel to the high water-mark. This is made of clay, strengthened towards the land with planks and stone; towards the water with rushes, sea-weed and flags, staked down, which give way to the force of the waves and resume their place again when they retire. Goldsmith has drawn a very elegant picture of the country in his admirable poem of the Traveller.

> "While the pent ocean rising o'er the pile,
> Sees an amphibious world beneath him smile,
> The slow canal, the yellow blossom'd vale,
> The willow tufted bank, the gliding sail,
> The crowded mart, the cultivated plain,
> A new creation rescued from his reign".[117]

It is wonderful that in a country without a stone or pebble, there should be stone edifices the most magnificent; without forests or an oak tree (two little woods excepted) the Dutch Navy is the second in the world; without arable land, they supply half Europe with corn; and with a tract of country scarce larger than an English county, they can raise men and money to make themselves of importance in the eyes of the first power of Christendom. Facts so extraordinary require explanation, I must beg you therefore to recollect that this state was founded on Liberty and Religion, was reared by Industry and Œconomy and has flourished by its Situation and Commerce. The bigoted maxims of Philip II[d], the introduction of the Inquisition and the erecting fourteen new Bishopricks in the Low Countries, the unrelenting rigour of Cardinal Granvelle, and the succeeding cruelty of the Duke of Alva, together with the Council of Twelve, called the Council of Blood, and the execution of Count Egmont and Horn, were the causes which drove the people to throw off the yoke and gave rise to the union of Utrecht.[118] Persevering valour, joined to the political assistance of other powers, have been the means of preserving their independence; while the decline of the Venetian Navy has made them the common carriers of Europe; and the wars in Flanders and situation of Holland have conspired to render Amsterdam the seat of universal commerce.

Till the beginning of the sixteenth century Venice by its shipping and Florence by its manufactories, possest the whole trade of Europe, Persia and the Indies; but the discovery of a passage to the East by the Cape of Good Hope and the settlements of the Portuguese in India proved fatal to the Republick of Venice; Lisbon then became the staple of trade to the East Indies, and the Easterlings who inhabited the Hans Towns were the great merchants of the North—they brought commerce first to Bruges and thence to Antwerp, which the Revolt of the Netherlands drew towards Holland.[119] The Dutch likewise in their success against the Portuguese in India and by their treaties with the natives, in process of time drew the whole trade of India from Lisbon.

Their situation is most admirably calculated for the trade of the Baltic, which includes Norway, Denmark, Sweden, Russia, Poland and the north coast of Germany; while they send merchandise into the interior part of the empire and the Austrian Netherlands by the Rhine, Maes and Scheld. You must likewise consider that each town values itself upon some particular branch of trade, by which it is improved to the utmost; as, for instance, Delft for the Dutch porcelain; Sardam for ship-building; Rotterdam for the Scotch and English trade; Amsterdam for that of the Streights, Spain and the East Indies; and the whole province for the Herring-Fishery which supplies the southern parts of Europe. Thus you see the greatness of this country has arisen from a wonderful concurrence of circumstances; from a long course of time, from the confluence of strangers driven either by persecution or invited by the credit of their government; from the cheapness of carriage by the convenience of the canals; from the low interest of money and dearness of land which consequently turn specie into trade; from particular traffick carried on at particular places; from the intense application to their Navy, from the vast nurseries for their sailors and from their amazing acquisition in the East-Indies: all these circumstances have conspired to make this little Republick the envy and admiration of the world.

Adieu!

Letter VII

Utrecht, Monday 14thAug.

Dear Sir,

We landed at Utrecht yesterday about three o'clock and a fine evening in some measure compensated for a rainy morning. This place is the capital of the province, situated on the channel of the old Rhine, called by the latin writers Trajectum ad Rhenum, thirty miles south-east of Amsterdam and twenty-five miles north-east of Rotterdam.[120] It is undoubtedly a most elegant town but without any public buildings to attract a stranger's notice. The houses are magnificent, the streets spacious and the environs delightful. It is larger than the Hague and is fortified with a rampart but untenable for an hour against a regular attack. In 1672 Louis XIV entered the town with his army without a shot being fired; kept possession of it for a twelvemonth and raised two hundred thousand pounds from the Inhabitants by way of contribution. In return to their complaisance Louis ordered his soldiers to spare the mall, which is the finest in Europe.[121] It is situated without the walls, is three quarters of a mile in length and has a treble row of trees on each side of the grand walk. You pass through a noble stone gate which leads to the mall and thro' a row of trees on the bank of the canal which encompasses the city. From the mall we mounted the dome, a tower belonging to the cathedral, now in ruins, which you ascend by four hundred and sixty steps. From this height is a vast prospect commanding fifty walled towns with the naked eye.[122]

The Oude-Graft (the old canal) is very spacious and crowded with vessels. The Nieue-Graft is inhabited by the noblesse. These two streets lie parallel to each other and are the finest both in point of extent, as well as in the grandeur of the houses. In the centre of the city is a pleasant grove of trees called St John's grove from the church which it surrounds.

Without the Amsterdam gate is a garden well worthy notice. It belongs at present to a widow lady.[123] It was made by a silk merchant at a vast expense. There are two costly grottoes and some excellent statues and vases by Jacob Crescant made in 1738 which are remarkable for the boldness of the basso relievo; Esther and Ahasuerus, Esther and Haman, David and Abigail, David and Saul in the care of Engedi are the stories of the relief.

The city has been rendered famous in history by the union of the seven provinces in 1579 whose deputies met here and framed that alliance which was the original constitution of the United Provinces and which was ever after called the union of Utrecht—a place that will be ever odious to an Englishman, from the ignominious treaty of 1713 called the Barrier Treaty by which Louis XIV was suffered to retain in his adversity the same advantages which he had reaped from the treaty of Ryswick in the zenith of his power; by which all the trading part of England was justly exasperated.[124] For, by the treaty of commerce, no higher customs were to be exacted from the commodities of France than from those of any other country which in the end must have ruined our trade with Portugal, at that time the most advantageous to Great Britain.

Pope Adrian VI has added dignity to Utrecht by claiming it as the place of his birth; the humblest, the worthiest pontiff that ever graced the Roman see.[125] He was an ecclesiastick of mean family and no interest but esteemed highly for his learning which induced the emperor Maximilian to appoint him preceptor to his grandson Charles V. He afterwards was regent of Spain and by the intrigues of the imperial ambassador, upon the death of Leo X was elected pope, tho' unacquainted with the manners of the people or the interests of the state and unknown to the persons who gave their suffrages in his Favour. His epitaph, written by himself, shews the temper and disposition of the man:

> "Adrianus sextus, hic situs est, qui nihil
> sibi infelicius in vitâ duxit, quam
> quod imperavit".[126]

But I am writing a letter not a history, therefore, lest you should accuse me of pedantry, I will instantly conclude myself sincerely,

Yours

Letter VIII

Breda, Tuesday the 15th

Dear Sir,

I wrote to you yesterday morning from Utrecht, which we left early; our mode of travelling is now changed in all respects for the worse. This is not the country to go post in, for we were obliged to hire a coach and four from Utrecht to convey us to Breda. The distance is only forty-two miles, notwithstanding which we were eleven hours on the road and paid five pounds sterling for this tedious, miserable conveyance. The country for the first twelve miles was rich and fruitful and extremely pleasing to the eye; but when we passed the Rhine, over which we were ferried, the prospect grew less agreeable, till we came at Golcombe, about twenty-four miles from Breda.[127]

Golcombe is a small town, surrounded with a rampart and a canal. The rampart is clothed with a fine verdure and shaded with a double row of trees which make the walk delightful. I saw nothing worthy a moment's notice except a line over an alms-house which breathed good christian charity in true monkish verse:

Da tua dum tua sunt, post mortem, tunc tua non sunt.[128]

Neither did I observe much appearance of trade which seems to me extraordinary as the Rhine runs so near and the Maes washes the town. The passage over it in a ferry boat with a sail is rather unpleasant. The distance I cannot judge of but we were above a quarter of an hour going over with a fair wind which bloweth rather too fresh for such a conveyance.

The country on this side of the Maes looked very dreary; wide uncultivated commons and heavy sands were all our prospect. On one of these commons, not far from Breda, the Prince of Orange had lately an encampment of ten thousand men which he reviewed in person. A few stakes and some sods of earth lay scattered over different parts of the common which we were told had been *Fortifications* at the grand review. They seemed to be counterparts of our infantile amusements on Blackheath and Wimbledon.[129]

We arrived here last night in time to take a little walk, while our dinner was preparing, for we had neither time nor accommodation to dine on the road; therefore we accumulated two meals by dining at ten o'clock at night. We were stopped at the gate on our entrance by an officer who demanded our names, quality &c., the first compliment of that kind we have been troubled with since our landing on the continent but the guards are ordered to let no stranger enter without being interrogated.

Breda* is the capital of Dutch Brabant and is under the dominance of the States general of the United Provinces; but it sends no deputies, neither is it under the control of any separate province but under the jurisdiction of the whole.[130] The established religion is the reformed, notwithstanding which the greatest part of the Inhabitants are catholicks. The fortifications are regular and the town is esteemed the strongest, except Bergen, on the Dutch frontiers.

The fortress is triangular, the ramparts are faced with stone and shaded with rows of elm, which extend entirely round the town. At every angle there is a gate built of brick. The curtains are flanked by fifteen bastions planted with cannon and by fourteen ravelins. It is about two miles in circumference. The country round is marshy and often overflowed by the river Merck. The fosse appears to be very wide and the water deep but the sentinels would not permit us to be very accurate in our observations.[131]

Near the market place stands the great church whose spire is three hundred and sixty feet high, from whose top you have a most extensive prospect commanding Antwerp to the South, at the distance of thirty miles, and Rotterdam about twenty-six miles to the North-West.[132] Within the church is the mausoleum of Anglebert the second Count of Nassau. He and his Countess are lying on a slab of black marble supported by four statues as large as the life, the arm of one and the leg and foot of another of these figures are transparent marble and much admired.[133]

---

* At this place the treaty between Charles II, Louis XIV and the States General was concluded in the year 1667. A treaty inglorious to England, which concluded a war wherein the two royal brothers were the only gainers; the king by pocketing the supplies granted by the commons for carrying on the war and the Duke of York by the present he had received from the parliament.

The castle is quadrangular, surrounded by the river Merck, is of brick and was built by King William.[134] It is adorned by busts of the most famous warriors and legislators among the Greeks and Romans. In the apartments is a great sameness, the rooms being either hung with tapestry or wainscoted with Norway oak on which there is some curious carving. The pictures are chiefly landscapes very modestly executed. Here are two good pictures of Venus. The one represents her lying on a couch and the three graces undressing the God of war; the carpet is astonishingly well done. The other is a Venus plucking a thorn from her foot; she is supported by Cupids, one of them in tears, is much admired. Adjoining to the castle are some fine gardens which belong to the States and are publick to the whole city.

There is nothing very striking in the town. The houses are old but not ruinous; the streets conveniently made, not spacious; and one canal only which, if I had not passed through towns crowded with them, I should have held in higher esteem. Our coach is at the door, therefore till I get to Bergen-op-Zoom I must bid you

Adieu!

Breda
Tuesday 3 o'clock
15 August

Letter IX

Dear Sir,

I left Breda yesterday afternoon in a coach and four which was six long hours conveying us twenty-one miles over deep sands and barren commons; about six miles from thence we passed thro' a neat, well-paved little town called Rosindale.[135] The morning has been spent in surveying the Fortifications of the place, for which purpose we rose at six o'clock.

Bergen-op-Zoom is the last and strongest fortress of Dutch Brabant. It is situated on an eminence in the middle of a morass, about a mile and a half from the eastern branch of the Scheld. The river Zoom runs thro' the town, whence it derives its name of the Hill on the Zoom. The town is small, the houses modern, being obliged to be rebuilt, the French in 1747 during the siege having levelled almost the whole town.[136] But the Fortifications are so extensive that they require ten thousand men to defend the works. We sent a card to the Commandant, who very obligingly ordered a sergeant and one of his own servants, who understood French, to show us the Fortifications. We wandered thro' the subterranean passages under the ramparts and were astonished at the ingenuity of Cohorn, the great Dutch engineer, who added such strong works to the Town that it is deemed impregnable by *Force*.[137] The side towards Antwerp is defended by a half-moon, whose trench is strengthened by four redoubts and by the river Escaut which communicates with the sea, whereby succours can be brought to the town in defiance of the besiegers. There are eleven forts between the town and the sea, with a great number of redoubts and palisadoes on the dyke. Under the ramparts are galleries of immense length, arched over, which extend to mines thirty-six feet beyond the palisadoes which are the outermost line of the fortifications. Such was its strength that it baffled two of the greatest Generals in the two last centuries; the Duke of Parma who unsuccessfully besieged it in 1588 and the marquis of Spinola who was obliged to raise the siege in 1622 with the loss of the flower of his army. At length it fell a victim to Count Lowendhall in 1747, or rather to the treachery of the Dutch Governor, the old Baron de Cronstrom, who ordered a captain's guard from the ravelin of Edem to another quarter and left there only a single sentinel, the consequence of which was that in a few hours after the French made good their ground on that very spot and forced the garrison to surrender.[138]

This anecdote I learned from the sergeant who attended us. He shewed us the very spot, assured me that he was one of the guard and spoke with that certainty of the fact that it left me no room to doubt; tho' our English historians impute it solely to the blind security the strength of the place had lulled the Governor into; while Voltaire, like a true Frenchman in his age of Louis XV, attributes it to the impetuosity and ardour of the besiegers which surmounted obstacles deemed insurmountable.

We purpose sleeping at Antwerp to night, from whence I hope to send you a more entertaining letter. Adieu! May the best wishes of your heart be servants to you.

Wednesday, 16 August

1. Harry Peckham's Bookplate

2. *Harry Peckham of the Markeaton Hunt* by Joseph Wright of Derby, *c.*1762

Above: 3. *The Young Bull* by Paulus Potter—"the flies on the cows seem alive"

Right: 4. Leiden, Bibliotheca Thysiana—"From the Academy you cross the road to the public library"

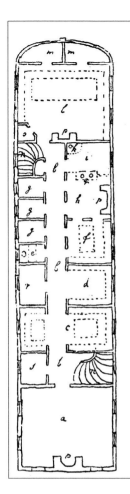

a) The States room hung with Damask
b. b. b) passage from end to end
c) a common room with 2 tables, open to yᵉ passage
d) another common room with benches only
e) a privey
f) a common room open to yᵉ Kitchen on one side & to yᵉ passage on the other
g. g) Store rooms & Larder &c
h) the Kitchen 7ᶠ Sqʳᵉ.
i) the scullery
k) the pump & sink
l) the best room for passengers 11 feet wide 13ᶠ long
m. m) Beds & cubbards.
n. n) Stairs
o) a beaufet
p. p. p) Chimnies
q) Stoves in the Kitchen

Left: 5. The Ghent–Bruges Draw Barge—"still more agreeable than the Dutch *trekschuyte*"

Below: 6. Lille, Porte de Paris—"most magnificent … but the entrance is contemptibly narrow"

7. *Christ on the Cross* by Van Dyck—"infinitely the best piece in Lille."

Above: 8. Lille—
entrance to the
Citadelle.

Left: 9. Paris, on the
boulevards—"places
of entertainment of
infinite variety."

10. *The Birth of Louis XIII* by Peter Paul Rubens—"The picture which struck me most" in the Luxembourgh Palace.

11. *View of the Chapel of the Chateau de Versailles.*

12. *General View of the Chateau and Pavilions at Marly .*

Letter X

Antwerp, Friday-night
18 August

Dear Sir,

I left Bergen soon after sending your letter on Wednesday and, on passing the gate, the guards did us the honour to turn out and salute. The same dreary wastes and heavy sands which have incommoded us from Golcombe continued till within a mile or two of this place; but I hear we have passed the Deserts and are now to be delighted with the fertile plains of Flanders. For these last two days I have made a toil of pleasure that I might reap the fruits of it on future recollections. At this moment I am weary and sleepy and my memory has not had time to digest what I have seen but as I know not when I shall be more at leisure must give you the best account I can.

Antwerp is the capital of the province whose name it bears, belonging to the Austrian Netherlands and under the dominion of the Empress Queen.[139] It is situated on the eastern shore of the Scheld, a noble river twenty feet deep at low water so that ships of great burthen may unload upon the quays or enter the town by eight canals which communicate with the river; some of which are large enough to contain a hundred ships at the same time.

The city is much decayed from its ancient grandeur, tho' it still remains a beautiful place. It is built in the form of a crescent, about seven miles in circumference, surrounded with a wall and bastions faced with stone; the top of the wall is a hundred feet broad with a double row of trees between which is a most agreeable walk. The streets are well paved, very spacious and uniform. The houses in general are seven or eight stories high, but old and in that miserable style of building which disgraces the towns in Holland. At the distance of a quarter of a mile is the Citadel, built by the Duke of Alva to keep the city in subjection. It stands on the banks of the Scheld and commands at once the river, the city and the adjacent country. It is built in a pentagonal form, with five bastions which defend each other, surrounded with double ditches.[140]

To this citadel is only one entrance which is over a draw-bridge. It is about a mile in circumference and well supplied with arms, ammunition and all warlike stores, with barracks for three thousand men. This fortress has been in such repute for strength and regularity that it has been a model for subsequent Engineers; notwithstanding which the French in 1746 took it in seven days.[141]

The trade of Antwerp is now confined within narrow limits, tho' so late as the sixteenth century there were two hundred thousand Inhabitants, two thousand five hundred ships lying often in the river at a time; and it was far from infrequent for five hundred vessels to come in or go out of the harbour in a day.

The trade of Antwerp in the year 1550, if the annals of their city can be relied on, amounted to one hundred and thirty-three millions of gold, without including the bank. As an instance of the amazing opulence of the merchants, there is a story upon record of John Daens a merchant who lent a million of gold to Charles V to carry on his wars in Hungary. The Emperor on his return dined with the merchant who gave him a most sumptuous entertainment and, at the close of it, burnt the contract by which the Emperor was bound to pay him a million of gold, in a fire of cinnamon which was the only fewel during the repast.

The rise of their trade was as rapid as the decline; and both proceeded from the same reasons. At the beginning of the sixteenth Century Bruges was the mart of Europe but the war at that time breaking out in Flanders the merchants withdrew from Bruges and were invited to Antwerp as a place of greater safety, the whole situation was happily calculated for commerce. But this did not last long for the civil wars breaking out in the Low Countries and Antwerp having twice been sacked, drove trade to a more peaceful refuge in Amsterdam.[142]

The established Religion is the Catholic; the Language low Dutch, but a bastard kind of French is talked by most of the Inhabitants. We lodge at the Grand Laboureur in the middle of the Mer street, called La place de Mer which I had the curiosity to measure and I found it to be fifty paces wide. It is much the most magnificent street I have ever seen. At the upper end is erected a crucifix, much admired by the connoisseurs.[143] We have been so fortunate as to see a grand procession in honour of St Rocque. The whole Mer was illuminated with torches and many hundred people in procession with flambeaux, followed by the Virgin Mary, precious relics, the host and an infinity of such like trumpery, amidst the chorus of voices, serpents and trumpets.[144]

There are a great number of magnificent churches in the city, full of valuable paintings by the great Flemish masters. Among these, the cathedral of Notre Dame has justly the pre-eminence. Yesterday, I spent the whole morning there and refreshed my memory again today with a cursory view. To mention all the pictures in this church which are worthy attention would fill a volume, I therefore must content myself with some few. The descent from the cross by Rubens is justly called his masterpiece, the position of the limbs of our Saviour is wonderful to behold; the varied expressions of the same passions in the different countenances of the weeping matrons surpass our imagination; all the figures are as big as life; among them he has introduced his three wives, his daughter and himself.[145]

The fall of the Angels, by Floris, ranks next in my esteem.[146] On the thigh of one of the fallen angels is a large hornet, painted by Quintin Matzys, the noted blacksmith of Antwerp, who fell in love with the daughter of Floris and demanded her in marriage; the painter refused him because he was not of his own profession. Matzys therefore changed his hammer for the pallet and studied under the Italian masters for two years. On his return he painted this hornet unknown to Floris, who by mistake was going to brush it off, thinking it alive. He was so pleased with the execution of it that he immediately gave his daughter in marriage. Matzys was buried on the outside of the western door of the church, where there is a plain stone with this epitaph:

Connubialis amor de mulcibre fecit Appelem[147]

I cannot omit mentioning a picture by Michael Coxie.[148] It represents St Ann surrounded with a vast group of women and naked children in attitudes the most pleasing. One little boy at his mother's breast it is impossible to forbear looking at. There is that pleasure and vivacity in his eye, mixed with an eagerness which nothing but the picture can give you an idea of.

The church is rich in marble as well as pictures, is five hundred feet by two hundred and thirty and the spire rises to the amazing height of four hundred and sixty-six feet and is esteemed the finest in the world.

The Town-house is a handsome square building with a fine portal which comprehends the five orders of architecture. Within are many excellent pictures, among them a game and fruit piece by Snyers, where is a bason of mulberries which cannot pass unobserved.[149]

From thence is a short step to the Jesuits church. The façade is enriched with statues and with other ornaments, under the direction and from the designs of the great Rubens. This church is a perfect piece of architecture, if tryed by the nicest rules. It is lined with marble throughout.[150]

The sodality is covered with pictures by Vandyke, Eyckens, Quillin and other capital masters.[151] The spaces between the pictures are lined with the richest marbles. Over the door is a much admired head of an angel in marble by Quillin which was saved from the ruins of the church when it was burnt down. The room under the sodality is well covered with pictures which you will find worth your seeing.

In the church of St Waldburge there is an excellent piece by Rubens over the altar, in three compartments. The history of it is the erection of the cross; the distress in the countenances of the Virgin and St John is strongly marked.[152]

The church of St James is remarkable for its size, for the tomb of Rubens who died in 1640 and for a picture of his painting in which he has portrayed himself under the figure of St George.[153]

The Exchange is an oblong square in the centre of four large streets; its size is a hundred and ninety-four by a hundred and fifty-four feet.[154] There is nothing striking in the building but you will find some good pictures in the saloon, at the end of which is a neat little Theatre where plays are acted during the carnival. Here likewise is the school of the Academicians where there are a great number of drawings which have been left by them who obtained the prizes. In the room adjacent is an excellent piece by Snyers, the bird's nest will point it out to you.

From thence we went to the Convent of the Carmelites. In the church is a chapel dedicated to the Virgin, with the roof arched, lined throughout with marble and enriched with a statue of the Virgin in massy silver, six feet and a half high.[155]

The grandest Convent in the city is the Dominicans.[156] The refectory is covered with pictures by Quillin, most admirably executed. There is a deception of a stair-case with a fish lying on one of the steps which must attract every eye. In the church is a grand piece by Rubens, the adoration of the magi; which he finished in thirteen days. The apartments of the abbot are well worthy of a prince, I know not a more magnificent place. Such a profusion of capital pictures by the best Flemish and Italian masters, with paintings to imitate basso relievo executed in a style to deceive an artist. Having seen everything that was curious, our valet carried us to the public Magazine where we were to be regaled, in his estimation, with the greatest curiosity in the city. You will be as much surprised as I was when I tell you there was nothing but some paste-board giants thirty feet high, with whales and elephants of the same materials, which are carried in procession thro' the streets on grand days. I can say nothing of their women for they entirely hide their faces with a kind of black veil. The better sort wear long white cloaks, with the heads so large that their faces were effectively concealed.

From your friend

18 August

.

Letter XI

Dear Sir,

We left Antwerp Saturday last at seven in the morning, dined at Mechlin, which is midway between Antwerp and Brussels; situated in the heart of Brabant, capital of the lordship of Mechlin, and was erected into an Archbishoprick in the sixteenth century by Paul IV. The primate's title is primate of the Low Countries.

Mechlin stands on the rivers Dyle and Demar which are united before they reach the city. The market place is spacious, the streets tolerably wide but the houses are old and vilely built, the fortifications are trifling and incapable of defence. The cathedral, dedicated to St Rombaud, is a fine Gothic structure in which is the Lord's Supper by Rubens.[157]

In St John's church there are two pictures of great value. The one is the Adoration of the Magi; the other is Herodias with St John's head in a charger; the satisfaction which appears in her countenance and the blood spouting from the trunk of the apostle are inimitably executed. Both these are by Rubens, as is the picture of St John in the act of being thrown into a caldron on boiling oil. These make three compartments over the grand altar.[158]

In the church of Notre Dame is another piece by the same master, of the Miraculous draught of Fishes. The attitudes of the fishermen are most admirable and their forms and faces so various that this picture alone would be sufficient proof that Rubens was no *Mannerist*.[159] The grand altar is of Egyptian marble, ornamented with a picture of the Last Supper.[160]

The Façade of the Jesuits church is the most beautiful in the city, the inside of it is likewise much esteemed as well for the pictures as for the elegance of the architecture.[161] The roof is oval supported by two rows of slight pillars.

After we had satisfied our curiosity and appetites we pursued our road to Brussels and passed thro' the little town of Vilvorden six miles from Mechlin and about the same distance from Brussels. It is a poor beggarly place, the certain consequence of too may religious houses with which the town is crowded. There are draw-boats which go from thence to Brussels in about an hour and a half.

The whole road from Antwerp is delightful; a spacious pavement, shrouded with double rows of trees; with the addition of the river Senne running by the road for the last six miles and the prospect enlivened by neat villas and pleasant gardens.[162]

We arrived at Brussels in time to dress and go to the Theatre which is much esteemed for its size and the elegance of its decorations. It was built by the Prince of Bavaria in the year 1700. Bellcour, the great French comedian, played in both pieces. He speaks well and acts with much ease and politeness.[163] He filled the part of the drunken marquis in the Retour imprévu with infinite applause.[164]

Some of the boxes resemble closets from which you see the stage but are invisible to the audience unless you chuse to sit forward. They have chimneys and it is not uncommon for the proprietors of these boxes, who are the first of the nobility, to have a dessert and wine for themselves and friends.

We have stayed for four days and it is so agreeable a place that it is with regret that I leave it tomorrow. The playhouse, especially when the actors are good, which they are here, is to me a great entertainment. There is likewise vast comfort in meeting agreeable people at the Table d' Hote which we always make a point to dine at, wherever we are, for the sake of improvement in the French language and to wear off, by a variety of company, that *mauvaise Honte* which so strongly marks the English.[165] We live at the Hotel l'Imperial with a chevalier of the Teutonic Order, a French abbé, a Dutch colonel and two English gentlemen; add to these a Venetian officer, an Italian who has served under the King of Prussia, with his daughter and an old duenna. The four last I take to be needy adventurers but they add not a little to our entertainment.

Brussels is the capital of Brabant and all the Austrian Netherlands, twenty four miles south of Antwerp and thirty south-east of Ghent, situated on the Senne, an inconsiderable river. The site of the city resembles Guilford

[sic] being built on the brow of a hill. Its figure is oval, about four miles in circumference, surrounded with a wall and tolerably fortified; the low town has the benefit of canals which admit boats of considerable burthen.

It is well supplied with fountains, some of which are rather whimsical, for instance, the three virgins from whose breasts flow continual streams of water: but to show you that the male sex is as charitably inclined there is a statue of a boy who spouts out water with most immodest assurance. The stream flows not from his *Breast*. It is called in the Flemish tongue *Mannykypis*.[166]

The streets are well paved and spacious; the houses in general, large and modern, owing to the bombardment of Marshall Villeroy in 1695 which reduced the town to a heap of rubbish.[167] The country around Brussels is most delightful to the eye and extremely profitable to the possessor, for the land within ten miles of the city sells at forty years purchase and lets in general for three pounds sterling per acre.

The churches are both in structure and elegance far inferior to those of Antwerp. The great church dedicated to St Gudula, situated on the hill near the gate of Louvain, is the most magnificent but greatly deformed by two misshapen towers at the West end.[168] Unluckily, the inside was cleaning and the pictures were removed which I heard were very capital. A monument near the great altar, erected to the memory of Ernest, Arch-duke of Austria and Governor of the Low Countries was the only recompense I received, there being nothing else to give one moment's pleasure.[169]

Near to the church are the remains of the palace which was accidentally burnt down about twenty years ago, situated in a pleasant little grove with some deer which the people pompously style the park.[170] One side of it is fenced with the ramparts. At a short distance is the arsenal which stands on the top of the street called Montagne à la Cour. There is some old trumpery armour in it, of neither curiosity nor use; except an iron shirt, which was worn by Charles V, that no sword can pierce; and a steel shield so finely engraved that the figures seem reflected from the polish, not to be etched in the steel. The nicest touch cannot perceive the least scratch, notwithstanding which, the figures appear to be strongly marked when the shield is held obliquely.

Just below the Arsenal is the Palace of Prince Charles of Lorraine, brother-in-law of the Empress and governor of the Austrian Netherlands. The present palace is not more than half finished.[171] There was upon this spot an old palace, which was bought of the Prince of Orange, at the time the grand palace was burnt, in which was a most capital collection of pictures, especially of Rubens, which with many valuable curiosities perished in the flames.

The stair-case of the present palace is very magnificent. The steps are of marble and the balustrade of iron gilt adorned with compartments of birds and beasts nicely executed in polished steel. The ceiling is painted in fresco.

The apartment of the Princess is hung with the Brussels tapestry, which is brought to great perfection tho', I think, unequal to the Gobelins. The floors are all inlaid with mahogany and box. The Princess's cabinet is much admired, being covered throughout with the finest japan. The Prince is a great mechanick and has a cabinet of curiosities, trifling enough, among which are two boxes containing all the common trades in miniature.

In the Menagerie I saw some fowls which were the produce of a very unnatural amour between a rabbit and a hen. They were of various sizes according to their age. Their breast and bellies clothed with white fur, their wings and backs covered with feathers without the plume which rose from the skin and had the appearance of wet feathers. They are all milk white as are their parents; their shape in every respect the same as other fowls. I saw the hen turned into the rabbit; the buck was amorous, the lady was not coy and they gave me repeated proofs of their happiness. The rabbit, like many husbands, has almost stript his wife of her clothing, having bit half the feathers from her back. I wonder not so much at this union as I every day in England see matches as unnatural.

From the menagerie we walked to the Mall or, as it is called the Alavert, situated just without the town on the Mechlin road. This is a genteel place for airing both on foot and in a carriage.[172] Here is a grand canal, with a mall on each side, without side of which is a road for carriages.

The Maison de Ville is a stone quadrangular building with a fine cupola.[173] Some of the apartments are ornamented with Brussels tapestry most admirably executed; Charles V resigning his crown to his son Philip, and an historical piece of Charlemagne, are framed and it must be an accurate eye to distinguish them from paintings, so lively are the colours and the features so expressive. In one part of the tapestry is introduced a curtain of crimson velvet which is so finely shaded that it seems to be real velvet. These two pieces are hung up in the States Chamber.

We got access to the cabinet of Mr ——— a private gentleman of a very whimsical turn. I had the honour of some conversation with him. He seems in perfect health but has not been out of his house for these twenty-three years, thinking that the open air would be instant death to him. His collection of pictures is most superb. A landscape and two hermits by Teniers are remarkable, as is a snow piece by the same hand where the snow is actually falling which I never saw attempted before. Teniers in this piece has not sufficiently studied nature for he has made the falling snow white; in fact it has not that appearance in the horizon for it looks black till parallel with some opaque object.[174] The Purification by Carrachi[175]—Our Saviour and the Man struck with the Palsy by Vandyke—An Old Man by Titian—Rembrandt by himself—A game piece by Snyers, in which there is a hedgehog, alive I believe but I was afraid to satisfy my doubts lest it should prick my fingers.

In a little room with glass doors is an original piece by Rubens in which are painted his three wives. The history of it is from the new Testament. It was purchased by this gentleman for two thousand guineas. In the same apartment is an admirable Game-piece by Snyers and a Battle by Vandermulen with many other capital pieces.[176]

We leave this heavenly spot tomorrow morning to my great regret but our time is short therefore we must away.

Adieu!

Brussels, 23 August
Wednesday-night

Letter XII

Dear Sir,

I left Brussels early yesterday morning and breakfasted at Alost, a small town under the dominance of the Empress Queen; situated about fifteen miles from Brussels and the same distance from Ghent.[177]

You cannot employ your time better while your horses are baiting than by strolling into the great Church where is a good picture of the martyrdom of St Roque, said to be the work of Rubens. I should rather apprehend it came from Rubens's school, for tho' it is painted in his manner, it is much inferior to the works of that great master.[178] The martyrdom of St Ann is a picture too good to pass unobserved and the figure of the Turk is excellent.[179] The altar is neat; over it is the Lord's Supper in basso relievo on Italian marble.

In seeing the church you see everything at Alost; you must therefore proceed with me to Gand, or Ghent, where I arrived yesterday to dinner since which time I have seen those few things which merit the attention of a stranger.

Ghent* is a large town with spacious streets and regular buildings, strongly fortified but far inferior to my idea of the strength of it. There are two or three canals run thro' the town which contribute much to the beauty of the place as well as to the convenience of the Inhabitants.

---

*   This place gave birth to Charles V in the year 1500. He was the son of Philip the handsome, Archduke of Austria, whose parents were the Emperor Maximilian and Mary the only child of Charles the Bold, the last Prince of the House of Burgundy. His mother Johanna was the daughter of Ferdinand and Isabella, King and Queen of Castille and Arragon.

The Abby of St Pierre is infinitely beyond any thing in Ghent.[180] It is situated on rising ground at the extremity of the town and consists of an Abbot and thirty-seven Benedictine Monks. The refectory is superb and fitter for a palace than a convent. It is paved with black and white marble and painted throughout in a very masterly manner.

The Library is equally magnificent; the number of books are very considerable but I could see nothing but the fathers, consiliums, stuff and nonsense. There were some few of the classicks and two or three good dictionaries. The ceiling is painted in fresco and the walls over the book cases are painted in imitation of basso relievo. From the windows you have a most delightful as well as extensive view of the country. In the church is some tapestry held in great estimation which has been there upwards of two centuries. It contains the histories of St Peter and Paul in divers compartments, most admirably finished; it was the work of Croyer of Brussels. The horse in the conversion of St Paul is the finest animal I ever beheld. Our Saviour standing on tiptoe on a wave is the true sublime and is most happily executed. A king humiliating himself to St Benoit is finely done; but the pride and vanity of those idle religious appear for ever in their pictures, their tapestry, their writings and their actions.[181] Elimus struck with blindness has much merit; and a marble floor is as nicely imitated in the tapestry as I have ever seen in a picture.[182]

In the church is a crucifixion by Vandyke which is greatly valued. The dome is small but well proportioned.[183]

The abbot's house is most sumptuous. Prince Charles of Lorrain always resides in it when at Ghent.[184] The apartments are crowded with good pictures but three by Rubens are most excellent. The one is Joseph with the infant Christ in his arms, two others are the heads of old men. One room is hung with tapestry by Oudenard, describing the history of Don Quixote; the colours are lively and the figures well proportioned but unequal to the same history at the King of France's palace at Marli.[185] In the chapel is a picture of King David on his death bed, with his son Solomon standing by him. This picture is done by Sarkall, a young man about thirty years of age who lives in this town and promises to be a very capital painter.

The Cathedral is a noble old building dedicated to St Buvon, of whom there is a good statue over the grand altar standing on the clouds which are supported by angels.[186] Against the pillars of the church are fixed some tolerable statues and, where there were vacancies, they have painted figures in imitation of statues so happily that it is difficult at a distance to find out the deception.[187] The pulpit is said to be the grandest of the kind; it is of marble enriched with statues and has two angels to support the sounding-board.[188] There is a capital picture of St Buvon by Rubens in which he has introduced himself, his wife and Family.[189]

The monument of Bishop Trieste by Fiamingo is most admirably executed; the boys do not yield even to those of Cardinal Richelieu's monument at the Sorbonne.[190] Fiamingo's principal excellence was in boys and the delicate. He had the art of softening and vivifying his marble to a surprising degree. In this respect he was the superior to Michael Angelo, who attained the antique only in strong muscular figures not in those of youth, nor women who under his bold hand grew Amazons.[191] The Maison de Ville has two fronts, the one in the gothic the other in the Grecian style, of three stories, adorned with attic, ionic and corinthian columns. There are some few fine pictures, as the day of Judgement by Rubens and the Coronation of Charles V in which picture are five hundred figures, most of them taken from life.[192] But the most capital picture is Hercules between Virtue and pleasure taken from Cebes's table; I could not learn the name of the master.[193]

There is a neat little convent in which the English ladies are immured. I saw a nun whose family live near Worcester ringing the bell for prayers; her veil accidentally flew back and discovered a face which would have charmed an anchorite.[194] Such a girl seemed better calculated for less pious uses. I am just summoned to breakfast; as soon as finished must quit this place and proceed to Bruges.

I am, yours &c.

Friday Morn 25 Aug
Ghent

Letter XIII

Dear Sir,

We left Ghent yesterday morning in a large boat drawn by two horses. This was still more agreeable than the Dutch trekschuyte, as it has an awning over the end of the deck where you may sit very much at your ease.[195] Below there are two separate apartments, the one elegantly fitted up for the better sort of people; add to these a kitchen where they dress you a good dinner at so much a head.[196] I don't remember spending a more agreeable day, the weather particularly fine, the view of the country delightful, joined to the conversation of a very pretty French woman who was lively and good humoured to a degree. We arrived here early in the evening and strolled round the town. In our walk we encountered an English lady who is married to a native of Bruges, by profession a lawyer. She invited us to her house with excess of civility; shewed us a small but good collection of pictures, gave us some excellent wine and loaded us with fruit from her own garden.

To-day we have surveyed the town more accurately. It is situated in Flanders and belongs to the Empress Queen; indeed the whole ten provinces often pass by the name of Flanders, in the same manner as the United Provinces are called Holland. It is fortified but seems of inconsiderable strength; the streets are wide and the houses tolerably built, but old; no trade nor even the appearance of traffick to be seen but remains a miserable monument of its ancient grandeur.

The place for the grand guard is a tolerable square, on one side of which is the Guard-House, ornamented with colonnades which have a pretty effect.

We roamed thro' many churches but found very little entertainment. In the church dedicated to St Salvator is one good statue and many bad pictures.[197] In the cathedral they shewed us a *veritable* Rubens. It may have been touched by him but nothing more; the picture is not bad but you may judge of it yourself by looking over the great altar. In this church there is the picture of a dying man receiving the sacrament which has much merit.[198] The Jesuits church is a fine building; the isles [sic] are divided by a double row of pillars and the nave is separated from the altar by a balustrade of Italian marble, most curiously wrought with many figures of birds, beasts and men.

In the bishop's palace there is some good tapestry but nothing else worthy of notice.

In the English nunnery there is a very neat little chapel; the altar is composed of various kinds of marble curiously inlaid.[199] The nun who attended us has not taken the vow of enclosure, she therefore was permitted to walk about the town in the business of the convent, a liberty she by no means coveted and, if she was sincere in what she said, she much regretted not having taken the severer vow.

The Maison de Ville is a notable Gothic structure and is a fine contrast to the college opposite which is a modern edifice of free stone.[200] These two buildings, with a church and some well-built houses compose a very handsome square.[201] Bruges was much too melancholy to make a longer stay in; we therefore took a coach which carried us to Courtray, a fortified town belonging to the Empress Queen. It is of considerable size with a spacious market place and good streets.

The choir of the great church of Notre Dame is richly adorned with marble, the sides and pillars being lined throughout at the expense of Menlenair, one of the present canons. Behind the great altar is the Elevation of the Cross by Rubens. The resignation in our Saviour's countenance, the nonchalance expressed in the faces of the elevators of the cross, with the grief of the other figures are most beautifully contrasted.[202]

The chief trade of the town is a Manufactory of napkins, I think they are called damask.

We left Courtray on Sunday morning and passed thro' Menin, the last town under the dominance of the Empress Queen. It is an inconsiderable place and very indifferently fortified.

We entered the dominions of the French King at a little village called Hallvin, where we were stopt till we had paid for a permit to enter the kingdom. Unless your servant is in the carriage he passes without a fee.

It is about eight miles from this place to Lisle,[203] the capital of French Flanders, a place most worthy the attention of a foreigner, whether in respect to the strength and extent of the fortifications or to the beauty and regularity of the buildings.

The town is surrounded with a treble ditch, the ramparts are faced with stone of enormous size, covered with cannon and full of mines.[204]

The houses are uniformly built, faced with free-stone and ornamented with sculpture. The streets are spacious, regular and well-paved. The Rue Royale, which runs from the citadel to the market-place, is perfectly straight, is a mile in extent and sixteen steps in width. La Rue de Malade, which leads to Paris, is equally spacious. At the end of this street is the most magnificent gate in Lisle.[205] It is ornamented with statues, the arch is boldly executed but the entrance is contemptibly narrow.

The Market-Place is divided by the Exchange which is built similar to our Royal Exchange but the cloisters are filled with shops of all kinds. The Market Place is a noble square, sufficiently large for eight thousand men to exercise, which they do every morning directly opposite my window.[206]

They tell me there are fifty churches in the city. I have been in many of them but find but few pictures of merit. In the chapel of Notre-Dame de la Trielle is a good picture of our Saviour scourged, the blood just starting from his back is finely expressed.[207] The choir is of marble and the body of the church is ornamented with some wooden statues excellently carved.

In the church of the Capuchins is the descent from the Cross, said to be by Rubens.[208] It is probably a copy of his famous picture at Antwerp, by one of his school but it is not equal to the master, neither can it be supposed that his genius would condescend to copy even a picture of his own.

In the chapel of the Recolets are three good pictures but the Crucifixion over the altar by Vandyke in infinitely the best piece in Lisle.[209] St Antoine by Rubens, in which there is an ass prostrate on the ground, cannot escape your notice.[210]

In the Jesuits church are no pictures, yet the elegance of the building is well worthy observation and four statues kneeling before the altar are of excellent workmanship.[211]

In the church of St Maurice is a good picture of St Druon.[212] A magnificent altar of marble and silver is all that is worth seeing in the church of St Augustin. The portal of the Dominican church is much admired. In the church of the Carmelites is a fine pulpit; the sounding board is supported by flying angels and ornamented with some basso relievo.[213]

We obtained leave of the commandant to walk around the ramparts of the citadel but we were attended by a guard who prevented our making observations. It is detached from the town, and is surrounded with a regular fortification which appears to be of great strength.[214]

From the citadel we visited the Hospital which is as spacious as magnificent.[215] It is founded for the support of old people and children, all of whom are employed, according to their strength and years, in making shoes, lace, clothes, spinning yarn and other manufactories which require more art than strength. In this hospital is shown a spurious picture of Rubens but had he lived till this time he could not have painted all the pictures attributed to him.

The Magazin de Blé is a large stone building and appears sufficiently spacious to contain as much corn as the city could consume in twelve months.[216]

We frequented the Theatre every evening which is far inferior to Brussels in size and ornament but I think the parts are better filled. Caron, who plays harlequin, is a good comic actor; his wife has much merit and is the first dancer on the stage. I was much pleased with the play to-night, it is called the Dissipateur in which there are some fine strokes of the pathetic between the honest servant and the ruined prodigal.[217] The farce was a laughable thing called the Sylphide.

We proceed to Paris to-morrow morning and, by way of variety, intend travelling in the diligence which is to convey us there in two days, tho' the distance is a hundred and fifty-six miles.

Adieu!

Tuesday night
29 August

Letter XIV

Dear Sir,

Having recovered from the fatigues of my journey, I will catch the present moment to give you some idea of the places which lie on the road from Lisle.

We breakfasted at Douay, a large town well fortified. The streets are spacious but the houses bad. The church is an handsome edifice with an elegant spire rising from a square tower.[218]

From thence we proceeded to Cambray to dinner, which is a strong fortified town in the province of Flanders, famous for its Cambrick manufactory. The choir of the Cathedral is worthy of your attention.[219] It is built entirely of marble, adorned with excellent basso relievo in brass, and the altar is enriched with much silver ornament. Adjoining to the church is the Archbishop's palace, an awkward old building.

Peronne was the next place we passed, situated on the river Somme in Picardy, it is called one of the keys of the kingdom. Our baggage would have undergone a severe scrutiny at the Douane or Custom-House if we had not taken off the edge of the officer's vigilance with a six livre piece.[220] We lodged at a little dirty cabaret, for it deserved not the name of an inn, where we met with very indifferent accommodations, did not therefore regret the early summons of the coachman but proceeded soon after mid-night on our journey in which we found nothing entertaining until our arrival at Senlis, which is built on the side of a hill and watered by a little rivulet called Manette.[221] There are some ruinous fortifications and remains of a castle, said to be the work of the Romans.

The King was hunting in the neighbourhood and was to return thro' the town to Versailles in the evening.[222] So careful were the inhabitants of their

Grand Monarque that all the signs were removed, least peradventure they might fall on the royal Pate. There were reliefs of carriages and guards, at the distance of every six miles, waiting on the road which was covered with his numerous retinue. It had more the appearance of a triumphal entry than a return from partridge shooting.

The common Fields on each side of the road were full of Game who enjoyed perfect freedom in this land of slavery and were so tame that they would scarce move out of the way of the carriages.[223]

We arrived at Paris at six in the evening and had no reason to regret having travelled in the diligence as by it we avoided the insolence of the Post-Masters and squabbles of the Postilions who, like the barren womb, are never satisfied and say not it is enough.

In respect to our company, we had much reason to be pleased, having only three officers of infantry and an open-hearted priest who seemed to care very little about the hows and whens of life. Their behaviour was civil and their conversation lively and entertaining.

After having disengaged ourselves from the officious impertinence of porters and valets, who surrounded us the moment we descended from the coach, and having obtained a permit from the searchers of the Custom-House to take away our baggage, we drove to the Hotel de l'Imperatrice in the Rue Jacob where we have an elegant dining room with two bed chambers on the first floor and a bedchamber in the entresol, with an apartment for the servant, for three guineas per week.[224] I confess the lodgings are dear but the situation is good and the furniture magnificent. Add to this that Mademoiselle Brunett is young, sprightly and handsome, and her father keeps a number of carriages for hire, by which means our coach is always ready. We pay him half a guinea a day for it and a shilling for the coachman. We have likewise a valet de place who goes behind the coach, runs in errands and cheats us when he can.[225]

We generally dine at a Table d'Hote, where we find genteel people and good dinners. The price is different at different houses but for forty sous a head, which is twenty pence English, we dine most sumptuously on two courses of seven and five, with a dessert and a pint of burgundy; when ten are seated at the table it is full.[226] We always sup at home. We buy our wine of the merchant and our supper is sent from the neighbouring traiteurs.

Having thus told you how I live in my next I will endeavour to give you a good idea of this seat of dissipation but cannot conclude my letter without telling you I called this morning on Dom. Le P —— des Blancs-Manteaux, a monk I formerly was acquainted with in one of the provinces.[227]

He shewed me his study which consisted chiefly of the fathers in Latin. He confessed his ignorance of the Greek tongue and asserted that the Latin version, even of the New Testament, was better than the original.

Having rummaged over the dusty fathers, he shewed me his Holy of Holies, which was a little cabinet in which were the fathers of gallantry— Tibullus, Ovid, Petronius Arbiter &c. Here I found the original letters of Abelard and Eloisa; with which was bound up an epistle from Foulques, Prior of Dueil to console his friend Abelard *on his loss.* The title of it is "Epistola Fulconis Prioris de Diogillo" which concludes in these remarkable words:

> Christus omnia, quae perditisti, *multipliciter* et *mirabiliter*
> reformabit in glorificatione corporum in futuro beatorum; ac
> tum demum regula dialecticorum falsa apparebit, dicentium
> "in habitum nunquam posse redire privationem".[228]

Had this consolation been addressed to a Mussulman the mirabiliter and mutlipliciter would have been well calculated for the virgins of Mahomet's paradise; but that such kind of comfort should be administered by a prior to a monk induces one to think as uncharitably of the purity and wisdom of the Roman Catholic professors in the twelfth century as the Latin fathers and obscene authors in the Benedictine's study obliged me to judge of him today.

Adieu!

Rue Jacob
4 Sept.

Letter XV

Dear Sir,

I mean to confine myself in this letter within the walls of Paris and happy shall I esteem myself if I can give you a general idea of the place so highly spoken of by Frenchmen and so much resorted to by the English. It is situated in the Isle of France about two hundred miles south of Calais and one-hundred and twenty south-east of Dieppe. Its form is circular and surrounded with a wall. The ramparts, or boulevards, which extend more than half round the city, are ornamented with rows of trees, in the center of which is a spacious road for carriages and, on each side, shady walks. During the summer season these walks are crowded with the Bourgeois and the road with coaches. On the edge of the walls are coffee houses and places of entertainment of infinite variety. Singing and musick, both French and Italian, dwarfs and giants, conjurors and drolls, plays and rope-dancing with a thousand other articles of merriment to amuse both the eye and ear. But Vauxhall seems at present to be the place of most fashionable resort.[229] It is a new building situated on the boulevards, partaking both of Vauxhall and Ranelagh, but far inferior to either. There is a rotund, about the fourth part as large as Ranelagh, decorated with lustres, mirrors and pillars painted with wreaths of flowers. In the center, dancing masters, whores and children amuse themselves and the company in dancing cotillions, minuets, allemands &c. This building is separated from some large rooms by a gravel-walk of forty or fifty yards in length, on each side of which is a piazza filled with shops finely illuminated. In the middle of the walk is a lofty mast or may-pole, which men clad in sailors' habits are perpetually climbing up and again sliding down whether to entertain themselves or the company I am yet to learn.

These different species of entertainment continue and are frequented from five in the evening till two or three in the morning. The hard-working artizan soon disappears and the industrious tradesman in an hour or two after makes way for the people of fashion who call midnight the polite hour for the humours of the boulevards.

Having mentioned the situation, let me endeavour to guess at the size of Paris. I have walked round it, I have viewed it from the top of Notre-Dame and I cannot be induced to think that it is more than half as large as London and Westminster, including the suburbs.[230] But I must observe that the streets are contemptibly narrow; few equal to Drury Lane, the generality inferior to the narrow part of the Strand. Add to this that the houses are six or seven stories high and many of them inhabited by as many different families, which will account for the population of the metropolis. Yet there is much ground unbuilt on; for the noblesse have court-yards in front, surrounded with high walls and behind most of them are spacious gardens. The river Seine too, which nearly divides the city, branches off with little arms through many parts of the town and, though small in itself yet, upon the whole, must cover a considerable extent of ground. Over this river are thrown thirty bridges, which add much to the convenience of the inhabitants, though but little to the ornament of the place. The Pont-neuf is the most esteemed, which in fact is as pitiful as the river it is built over.[231] This bridge consists of eight arches. In the centre is a large bastion, erected on a point of land from whence the river divides itself into two branches, so that, in reality, this boasted nothingness is two bridges joined together by a mole of stone. On the middle of the pier is an equestrian statue of Henry the Fourth, very finely executed by Dupré; the horse is particularly admired which is by John Bologna.[232] Almost at the north end of the bridge is a four-square building called the Samaritain, which is a reservoir for supplying the pipes with water which communicate to different fountains in the city.[233] About two hundred yards up the stream you see the Pont-Mitchel which is covered with houses; about the same distance down the river you have a view of the Port-royal, the most modern and, in my opinion, the most beautiful bridge in Paris.[234] But it consists only of five arches and cannot be put in any degree of comparison with Westminster-bridge, even in point of elegance, much less of magnificence. Having mentioned the number of arches of these, the two grandest bridges, you may have some idea of the narrowness of the river, which is made still less useful by a number of shoals and the sand banks in many places appear above the water. There is nothing to be seen but a few little wherries and some house-boats of the larger kind, fixed in particular parts for the use either of bathing or washing of linen. These circumstances induce me to look on the quays that are erected on each side of the river as things rather of ornament than use. I must confess the banks being faced with stone and the parallel streets with handsome fronts towards the water have a very fine effect especially when compared with the banks of the Thames, edged with coal-wharves and timber yards.[235]

Having spoken of the river, I will now mention the gates of Paris, four of which merit the attention of a stranger, as they were built for triumphal arches to perpetuate the victories of Louis XIV. I mean the gates of St Antoine, St Bernard, St Martin and St Dennis, which is much superior to the other three being seventy-two feet high and adorned with excellent basso-relievo, the one side representing the passage of the Rhine, the other the taking of Maestricht.[236] Within these gates are four royal palaces in which neither the King, nor any of the royal family ever reside. In truth, the first I mention, which is called the Palace, cannot accommodate a monarch: it is like our Westminster-hall, appropriated to the same purposes, for the parliament, for the chamber of accounts and for other courts of justice.[237] The passages, or rather halls, which lead to these different courts are an object of curiosity by the infinite variety of toys and knick-knacks which are offered to your notice by the mistresses of these little shops who attack you as you pass with, now and then a word of English and with such an inundation of French that a man must have more than legal impudence to run the gauntlet through such a number of chattering females.

The Luxembourgh was built by Mary of Medicis, wife of Henry IV and mother of Louis XIII.[238] It describes a quadrangle and resembles the front of Queen's-college in Oxford, having a colonnade with a dome in the center under which you enter the court. The first story is of the Tuscan order, above are the Doric and Ionic. The whole is extremely elegant but the pictures within are the most worthy admiration, especially the Luxembourgh gallery, painted by Rubens in twenty-four large pieces in which this great master has comprized the history of Mary de Medicis.[239] You see these valuable pictures to very great disadvantage, the gallery being too small for their size and the light is so bad that not even a connoisseur can determine on their merit. The picture which struck me most represented the Queen, sitting in a chair as just delivered of her son, her face strongly marked with the agony of pain she had so lately undergone, mixed with a look of inexpressible fondness for the child, on which her eyes seem riveted.

There are three other rooms open to strangers, in which are pictures of the most capital masters. Those that more immediately attracted my eye were a picture of Charity, under the figure of a woman employed in taking care of some little children. This was originally painted on wood, which decayed, and Mr Ricault took off the painting and fixed it on canvas in so exact a manner that the most observing eye cannot discern that it was not originally painted on it.[240]

The Rape of the Sabines by Nic. Poussin.[241]

A Roman Charity, by Guido; in which the light thrown on the face and breast cannot escape you.[242]

The Musicians by Francis Puget; among which the famous Lully is distinguished by pointing to the music-book.[243]

Abigail before David, by Veugle.

Job and his family prostrate before the angel who is ascending to heaven; by Rembrandt.[244]

The infant Jesus, the Virgin and St John by Raphael; the best picture in the whole collection.[245]

Our Saviour driving the money-changers out of the temple is a very large and capital performance. The scene of confusion is highly finished. In this piece is happily introduced a boy with a cage of doves, the door of which is described as open; the doubt and anxiety in his countenance, whether he should catch at the dove as it is escaping or put his hand on the door to detain the others is happily executed. But there is no meaning in our Saviour's countenance; for by endeavouring to paint his meekness and humility, the artist has given him a face void of all expression.

These paintings may be seen gratis every Wednesday and Saturday, from four till seven in the evening.

From the Luxembourgh palace I must take you to the Louvre, begun by Francis the First and continued down by different princes but still remains unfinished. The grand façade towards the river can never be enough admired.[246] On the first story is a gallery, formed with twenty-eight pillars, which sustain architraves twelve feet long. These are much admired, especially for the leaves in the chapiters.[247] This front is of immense length and has a noble effect from the opposite side of the Seine. The quadrangle at the east end is now repairing and it is the design of the present King to complete this magnificent palace.*[248] The apartments are given to artists of the first eminence to dwell in.

In this palace is the annual exhibition of pictures, which I have viewed with some degree of attention but they are in no respect comparable to the performances of the English artists.[249] In the choice of their subjects there is

---

* Bethlem is built in imitation of the east front of the Louvre.

much imagination but their colours are glaring and instead of nature you have only the tinsel of art.

This palace is joined to the Tuilleries by a long gallery in which are preserved plans of all the fortified towns in France and of the principal fortifications of Europe. I have heard they are extremely curious but they are hid from the public eye.

The last royal palace is the palace of the Tuilleries, began by Mary de Medicis, continued by Henry IV and finished by Louis XIV under the direction of the great Colbert.[250] The front is three hundred and twenty-six yards long, having three courts on one side, on the other the gardens. The grand façade towards the gardens consists of five pavilions; the center is adorned with the Ionic, Corinthian and Composite orders, with an Attic. The columns of marble are fluted and filled up with olive branches which give it an inconceivable richness. The gardens are resorted to in the evening by all ranks of people, where are an infinite number of benches to accommodate the idle and infirm. These gardens are laid out with the greatest regularity, designed by Le Nostre [sic], a name more famous in France than Capability Brown in England. The grand terrace is five hundred and sixty yards long, by twenty-eight broad, shaded with a double row of trees. It is parallel with the river, of which, and of the town, you have a fine view from this walk. The parterres are adorned with marble statues of admirable workmanship; and round the grand bason, at the extremity of the principal walk, are the four rivers personified, of colossal stature, reclining on marble pedestals, the whole most wonderfully executed. The Seine is by De Coustou, the Loire by Vaneleve; the Tyber and Nile are copies from the antiques at Rome.[251] Towards the bottom of the gardens is a thick grove of trees which in the day-time secures you from the sun and in the evening from the eye of observation; for, as soon as it is dark, every species of indecency is committed under those trees, far out-doing the bird-cage walk, the dark walk at Vauxhall or Ranelagh gardens. All elegant as are these gardens, yet so little care is taken of them and so little conversant are the French in cleanliness that one walk which is over-hung with a Yew hedge will give you ten thousand instances of filthiness.[252]

Next to the King's palaces the Palace-royal must be mentioned which belongs to, and is the usual residence of, the Duke of Orleans. It was built by Cardinal Richelieu and by him presented to Louis XIV who gave it to the Duke of Orleans, his illegitimate son.[253]

The palace is in the neighbourhood of the Louvre. Its outward appearance does not give that idea of princely magnificence which you find in all the apartments. In every room you see bronzes in the highest perfection, copied from the most beautiful antiques-tables inlaid with marble, porphyry &c.—cabinets of the rarest workmanship, china jars of extraordinary excellence, lustres of rock crystal and an infinity of things worthy admiration. But these are nothing compared to the collection of capital paintings which is infinitely superior to any collection I have seen; and I have heard it advanced by connoisseurs who have made the grand tour that it is not equalled in Europe. Among such numbers I can scarcely tell you what I most admire, though I have been twice to feast my eyes on them.

The gallery, called the gallery of Aeneas, from his history in fourteen large pieces most inimitably done by Coypel, will attract your notice.[254] This, like the Luxembourgh gallery, is too small for the size of the pictures and is much out of proportion, being neither wide nor lofty enough for its length. The saloon does the architect much more credit; this is covered with excellent pieces of the best Italian masters. I will mention some few in the different parts of the house which gave me the greatest satisfaction.

Mars and Venus tied together by a little Cupid with chains of flowers— P. Veronese.[255]

The death of Adonis: Venus weeping over him, with Cupid falling headlong from a tree in the back ground—P. Veronese.

Joseph and Potiphar's wife, painted on brass; the varnish is wonderful. By Alexander Veronese.[256]

God the father sitting on the many-headed monster with his arms supported by two angels. By Raphael.

The Virgin with our Saviour and St John, esteemed the most capital in the whole collection, by Raphael. This is a very small picture in a gloomy room, therefore may be passed over unobserved.

A holy family: the Virgin holding the infant Jesus in her arms, Isaac standing by looking on the child with an earnestness and satisfaction that makes you almost forget it is a picture. By Raphael.

The martyrdom of St Hippolita with her face pinched with red-hot pincers; St Sebastian transfixed with arrows with his hands tied to a tree. Two capital pieces by Guido.

A holy family but unequal to Raphael's by Carrachi.

St John looking at our Saviour who stands on a distant mountain. Carrachi.

The baptism of our Saviour by Albani.[257]

Alexander sitting by his bed, with the bowl in his hand, his physician standing by him.* The intrepid confidence in the eye of Alexander and the conscious integrity that marks the countenance of Philip force me to give this piece the preference to the whole. It is the work of Le Soeur.[258]

Moses striking the rock. By Poussin.

Cupid bending his bow, with two little Cupids playing between his legs, the one crying for being trod on, the other laughing at his misfortune. By Corregio.[259]

Heraclitus and Democritus, two large pieces, finely contrasted. By Hispanioletti.

Venus bathing, standing up to the knees only in water, the golden tresses flowing negligently on her neck. By Titian. She is indeed a goddess for never was such a woman blessed with such symmetry, such beauty. If you may judge of the man from the painter, Titian indisputably had the most wanton imagination of all artists, for you see *nakedness* in almost every piece of his; but then it is such a nakedness that the eye of modesty would not wish clothed.[260]

From one of the apartments, a door communicates to the Duke's lodge in the new opera-house which is adjoining to one end of the palace. No one but a Frenchman would chuse to have such a riot, noise and uproar close to his very doors which must be the case when the opera is opened; but it is not yet finished.

The gardens belonging to the palace are neither very extensive nor very elegant, yet from twelve to two, in the summer season, you will meet there all the beau monde. It is the fashion and nothing but the shady walk in the Palais-Royal gardens is resorted to at that time of the day, though both the Luxembourgh and the Tuileries are infinitely more shady and more pleasant.

The Bourbon palace (Rue de l'Université) belonging to the Prince of Condé, was built by his grandmother (the natural daughter of Louis XIV) in the Italian style, being only one story high.[261] It describes a semi-circle with two large wings joined to it. The statues of Minerva and Plenty, the architecture and the view of the Seine from the windows make it worthy to be the residence of a prince. But it is not at present inhabited, vast additions being intended which an infinite number of workmen are executing with all possible dispatch.

I did not think it half an hour thrown away in seeing the hotel of the Duc de V———, son of the famous Marshall who gained so many laurels in

---

* Alexander being ill, Philip the Arcanian offered to administer physick to him; at the same time Parmenio wrote him word that Philip was bribed by Darius to poison him. Philip attended the king with the potion, which Alexander immediately swallowed, at the same time putting into his hand the letter of accusation he had received. This is the story on which the picture is founded.

Louis XIV's time; but, as Hamlet says, no more to be compared to him than I to Hercules—laurels grow not in the barren soil of Sodom.[262] In this house are some good pictures of his father's battles; but the gallery is chiefly to be admired; it is almost covered with pier-glasses of the largest size; the cornice and ceiling all gilt in the richest manner and over every glass is the picture of a woman, each in a different attitude; very pleasing, tho' not perhaps strictly decent.

Mr Blondel, in the Place de Vendome, has a very capital collection of pictures for a private gentleman which is much esteemed and is visible to all strangers.[263]

I have now, to the best of my recollection, given you an account of those palaces and houses which are most curious. Among such a variety of things which I have still to mention, I scarce know which first to carry to your attention but must take you, I believe from the house of man to the house of God. I therefore shall begin with Nôtre Dame, which is the cathedral, of gothic architecture built in the form of a cross, one hundred and thirty yards long, forty-eight broad and about forty yards in height; the whole supported by one hundred and twenty beautiful pillars. In front of the church are three large gates, adorned with a number of figures in basso-relievo. Over the gates of the portal is a gallery embellished with twenty-eight statues of kings of France, from Childebert down to Philip Augustus.[264] The true Gothic magnificence shines forth in this portal, on which are two very clumsy towers; one of these I ascended and the very distinct view I had from it of Paris was an ample recompence. Immediately on entering the church you are struck with a colossal statue of St Christopher carrying the infant Christ on his shoulders.[265] This statue is twenty-eight feet high, hewn out of a rock; an odd ornament for a church. Here you find an equestrian statue of Philip le Bel, armed cap-a-pie as at the battle of Mons, which you probably will think as great an impropriety as the holy giant. In this church are many good pictures among numberless bad ones. In the choir are eight grand pieces, very finely executed by Coypel, Jouvenet and other great masters.[266] But the magnificence of the high altar is chiefly admired. It stands by itself in the centre of the sanctuary; the massive part is of marble, carved in form of an antique tomb. The sides are of porphyry, the front of brass, richly gilt, adorned with cherubims and two angels of larger proportion, in the attitude of adoration, born upon clouds and supported by pedestals of white marble.[267] In a niche is a group of four figures—white marble—The Virgin Mary sits in the middle, her arm extended, her eyes towards heaven; the head and part of the body of her son reclining on her knees. The rest of the body is stretched out on a winding sheet; a kneeling angel, with wings half extended, supports one hand of our Saviour, while the other angel holds the crown of thorns. This group is indeed of admirable beauty.[268]

In the treasury are vast quantities of trumpery-relicks and some few valuable curiosities, among which was a knife with these words on the hast: "Hic cultellus fuit fulcheri de Buolo, per quem Wido dedit areas drogonis Archidiaconi ecclesiae sanctae mariae, ante eandem ecclesiam sitas".[269] This knife is the title by which the canons hold an estate of six thousand livres per annum. There was likewise a small bit of wood with a Latin inscription giving by it certain lands to the church.[270] How easy in those days (1094) was the transferring of property when four inches square of wood answered the end of forty skins of parchment and a carpenter could as effectively make a conveyance of an estate as the first lawyer in the kingdom!

The hearts of Louis XIII and XIV are interred in the choir—their statues are in marble, kneeling on the right and left of the grand altar.

As Notre Dame is remarkable for the old Gothic magnificence, the church of St Sulpice is no less so in the Grecian style. The grand portal offers to your eyes a double row of Corinthian pillars; above are sixty-eight columns of the Doric and Ionic orders; to the right and left are two octagon towers. But the noble front cannot be seen to advantage by reason of the high wall of the seminary adjoining, which I hear is to be taken down to open the view; if not vast sums of money have been expended to little purpose.[271]

In the inside of the church the architecture is chiefly to be admired, together with six noble pictures by Vanloo.[272] The monument of Languet de Guerchy, Doctor of the Sorbonne, is happily designed. Immortality is pushing away Death who is in the act of covering the statue of Languet.[273] There is likewise a fine monument to the memory of the Dutchess of Lauraguais.[274] The canopy over the high altar is richly gilt and has a fine effect from the entrance of the church. There are two shells of uncommon size, given by Louis XV, which contain the holy water. They are called benitiers.[275]

As the church of St Roch (rue St Honoré) is the next in beauty, it shall next be spoken of.[276] It is a modern edifice, chiefly to be admired for the perspective of four chapels. The view is terminated with our Saviour on the cross which seems, from its situation, at a great distance; a window, properly disposed, throws the light exactly on the cross. The first chapel is dedicated to the Virgin of whom there is a fine marble statue in a kneeling attitude; the angel descending on a cloud and above are immense rays in gilding which give a wonderful magnificence.

In this church is a tolerable monument to the memory of that great philosopher Maupertuis; and an excellent picture of St Louis dying by Ant. Coypel: you will find it in a little chapel on the right of the choir.[277] I know nothing else worthy of admiration here, except the pulpit and the rails that separate the choir, which are of polished iron and of extraordinary workmanship.

Now I am in the rue St Honoré I will mention two or three churches in the neighbourhood and first that belonging to the convent of the Jacobins which is remarkable only for the tomb of Pierre Mignard, the celebrated French painter and for the monument erected to Marshall de Crequi, designed by Le Brun.[278]

But the church belonging to the Assumption, which is a convent of women, has many beauties worthy observation. It is built after the manner of the ancient pantheon in Rome which is now known by the name of St Mary's. A small dome comprizes the whole church which is extremely neat; the cupola is well painted in fresco by La Fosse, representing the assumption of the blessed Virgin.[279] There are some excellent pictures round the church, among which a crucifix by Ant. Coypel, the Flight from Egypt by Le Moine and a Holy Family by Boulogna have the greatest merit.[280]

At no great distance is the church of the Augustins Dechaussés which is built in the Ionic order. In the choir are seven large and exquisite pieces by Vanloo, giving the history of St Augustin.[281] Here is likewise the tomb of Lulli, the father of French musick, whose name I have already mentioned in a capital piece at the Luxembourgh palace.

I do not recollect any other church in this quarter of the town which merits attention; I must therefore take you to the other side of the river to admire the beauties of Val de Grace (Faubourg St Jacques) which is indisputably one of the grandest churches in Paris. It belongs to a female convent and was built by Anne of Austria, mother of Louis XIV.[282] The front is truely magnificent, with a great portico supported by Corinthian pillars and adorned with marble statues. On entering the church I know not which most to admire, whether the pavement of marble in different compartments, or the vaulted roof of inimitable sculpture in stone enriched with a great number of fine medallions, or the design of the grand altar which is as ingenious as magnificent. The canopy, on which is a crucifix, is supported by six twisted marble pillars, fixed in an oval form and ornamented with a gilt wreath. Under the canopy the child Jesus lies in a cloak, with the Virgin on one side and Joseph on the other, whose looks are expressive of the greatest humility, reverence and affection. These figures are in marble, big as the life and executed in a most masterly manner.[283] The dome is of just proportion, painted in fresco by Mignard, representing heaven opened. You see God the father in the middle, surrounded by saints and angels and Anne of Austria offering to the deity a plan of the church. I look on this as Mignard's masterpiece. In the elevated part of the dome the view seems to lose itself in infinite space.[284]

Almost opposite to Val de Grace is the church of the Carmelites, esteemed the most curious in Paris; of this order of nuns the queen herself was protectoress.[285] It is a little gaudy chapel, decorated in a profusion of gilding and pillars painted in imitation of marble. The sides of the chapel are almost totally covered with pictures of the greatest masters. On the roof is a picture of Christ in perspective, which attracts the attention of the curious; a Salutation by Guido is much esteemed. The altars are by Champagne, Stella, La Hire and Le Brun whose masterpiece is the picture of the Dutchess de la Valliere, mistress of Louis XIV who had the virtue at thirty years of age to prefer to the arms of a monarch this little convent where she retired when in the midst of all her glory and continued in it till her death which happened thirty-six years after.[286] Neither entreaties nor threats could prevail on her to return to the King and when he menaced to burn the convent to the ground, she replied, It would be a means of setting the other nuns at liberty but for herself she would rather perish in the flames. Her picture is in the character of a Magdalene, on her knees, her eyes red, swollen with tears, a drop trickling down her cheek, looking up to heaven, expressing the utmost contrition and penitence, with both horror and hope blended in her countenance; her jewels lie scattered at her feet; the inside of her left hand and her right hand and arm seem beyond the power of the pencil; and the picture taken together is one of the most capital I have ever seen.

In the same street is a miserable convent of English Benedictines, consisting of eighteen members. I saw some of them who appeared not to be more than twenty years of age. In this chapel lies in state that silly fellow James, not yet buried; for his followers, as weak as their master, think that the time will come when his family shall reign again in Britain; he therefore lies ready to be shipped off to England, to sleep with his ancestors in Westminster-abbey.[287]

The portal of St Gervais (quartier de la Gréve) is worthy attention, tho' it is so surrounded with houses that you can have but an indifferent view of it.[288] It is composed of the Doric, Ionic and Corinthian orders and is esteemed one of the finest pieces of architecture in Paris.

St Genevieve de la Couture (rue St Antoine) a church of regular canons, formerly belonging to the Jesuits; but the King, on their expulsion, gave it to the royal priory of Couture.[289] The ornaments on the outside of the church are rather heavy and confused. The inside is filled with monuments of fine sculpture.

In the little church of St Hippolite (fauxbourgh de Marcell), in my way to the Gobelins, I found some very tolerable pictures. I looked in by mere accident having never heard of this church before.[290]

The Holy Chapel adjoining the Palais Marchand is a small Gothic structure, much admired, built by St Louis. The windows are of stained glass; the colours remarkably lively, infinitely superior to the modern windows.[291]

I do not remember having seen any other church worthy your attention. I should therefore conclude this long letter but as the Sorbonne and the College of four nations are remarkable for their chapels, will finish with some account of them.

The Sorbonne was built by Cardinal Richelieu in which are apartments for thirty-six doctors who judge of the orthodoxy of publications.[292] But the Cardinal's intention was not, I doubt, so much the cause of religion as of vanity, to erect a building in which might be placed his monument. The church describes a cross and is paved with variegated marble. In the center of the choir is the tomb of the Cardinal, in marble, finely executed.[293] He reclines on a mattress, clothed in a loose robe of inimitable drapery. Religion supports his head, whilst Science sits weeping at his feet. The figures are as large as life and it is deemed the *chef d'oeuvre* of Girardon. The body of the Cardinal, with the mattress and the figure of Religion are all chissel'd out of one slab of marble.

The grand altar is likewise of marble, over which is a celestial glory, by Le Brun. In the chapel dedicated to the Virgin is her statue in stone, masterly done by Desjardins, or Martin de Jardin, who executed the statue of Louis XIV in the Place des Victoires.[294] You will find in a little adjoining chapel a picture of St Anthony preaching in the desert. He is seated in an armed chair, not a very common convenience in a desert, nor a very proper attitude for a preacher; but his hair is grey which I suppose to be an apology for his sitting. Coypel is the master and the piece does him credit.

I have now only to mention the College of four nations (rue Mazarin) built by Cardinal Mazarin and intended as a seminary for the education of children born in France, Picardy, Normandy and Germany.[295] The front forms a semi-circle, situated on the banks of the Seine opposite the Louvre. The building is in itself magnificent but chiefly admired for the chapel, the dome of which is remarkable for proportion and the contour. The mausoleum of the Cardinal is the work of Coysevox. He is represented on his knees, with bronze figures of Prudence, Abundance and Fidelity attending.[296] There are three pictures of Paul Veronese—the Circumcision over the grand altar is well preserved but the other two are totally spoiled.

There is a good library belonging to the college which is open on Mondays and Thursdays.

In my next will finish the description of Paris at present

Adieu

Paris 9th September

Letter XVI

Dear Sir,

I hoped to have brought the description of Paris within the compass of my last letter but there are so many particulars to be observed on that I am afraid you will think this letter long before I have finished the catalogue of the places *à voir*, as the French term it.

I must begin with the Hospital of the Invalids, founded by Lewis XIV for the accommodation of two hundred officers and three thousand soldiers who here find a tolerable subsistence when worn out with age and infirmities.[297] This building consists of five quadrangles of freestone, three stories high, surrounded with piazzas and open galleries over them which have a most magnificent effect. The greatest curiosity is the dome of the chapel, the noblest structure in the whole city.[298] The grand dome stands upon ten pillars of the Corinthian order, thirty-one feet in height. Above these columns are the four evangelists in fresco, painted by La Fosse. The roof is by Jouvenet in fresco likewise, exhibiting the twelve apostles with the instruments of their martyrdom. The cupola represents an infinite number of saints and angels adoring the glory in the center, where St Louis is offering his crown to God. This admirable piece of painting is by La Fosse.[299] This dome is surrounded with four others of inferior size but equal elegance. The pavement is of the choicest marbles inlaid with wonderful beauty. The grand altar is supported by six twisted columns covered with gold over which is a sumptuous canopy. Before the altar is St Louis washing the feet of a beggar in embroidery of needlework of divers colours. The pulpit is gilt in the richest manner; the pictures are indifferent, the Holy Trinity by Coypel is much the best.

From the hospital a grand walk leads to the Seine with rows of trees on each side. At a small distance is the Military School founded by the present king, for the education and maintenance of five hundred gentlemen's sons, among whom those are to have preference who have lost their fathers in battle.[300] At this place they are perfected in the military sciences who receive the rudiments of their education at La Fleche in the province of Mayenne.[301] Adjoining is the Campus Martius, an extensive plain surrounded with a fossé and treble row of trees. It is intended for the royal reviews and can accommodate eight thousand troops with space sufficient to exercise on.

This is at the south-western extremity of Paris from whence I must carry you to the south-east side to take a view of the royal manufactory of tapestry, called the Gobelins, Faubourg de St Marcell, which is superior to anything of the kind.[302] To describe their methods of working it is impossible. Instead of the threads being horizontal they are perpendicular. The artists copy pictures, which hang before them, with the minutest exactness, blending every tint with the various coloured worsteds as easily as the printer can with his pallet and brush. They work on the wrong side which makes it still more extraordinary; an infinity of bobbins hang from the work which they change as the picture requires with the greatest dispatch. The designs are chiefly historical and are done for the king.

There are many charitable foundations in this city, among which the most considerable is the Hospital General, which is said frequently to contain ten thousand people. It is composed of six distinct houses, into which the patients are placed, according to age, sex and infirmity.[303]

In the quarter of St Eustache is the Hall, a new building, lately finished at the expense of the city for the purpose of a granary and, it is said, can contain enough corn to supply the whole town for a twelve month. This building is circular, of freestone and has six gates which front as many different streets.[304] It is surrounded with a circle of houses whose fronts are of stone, all built in the same style of elegance and proportion.

There are only four squares in Paris, all inferior in point of size to Grosvenor Square but infinitely more elegant as the houses are of the same height and correspond with each other.[305] The Royal Square is the most ancient, built by Cardinal Richelieu to perpetuate the glory of Louis XIII in 1630.[306] It is surrounded by a piazza like Covent Garden. In the center is an equestrian statue of Louis XIII. The horse is much esteemed, the work of Daniel Ricciarelli; the king is by another hand.[307] The French say, to make a perfect equestrian statue Henry IVth must be placed on Louis XIII's horse. On the pedestal, which is of white marble, are four inscriptions in French and Latin, tending only to perpetuate the name of Richelieu, instead of recording the life of Louis the Just.

The next in priority of time is the place of victory built by the Duke de Feuillade in honour of Louis XIV in the year 1686.[308] The houses are in the Ionic style and describe a circle in the center of which is the statue of Louis XIV on foot, victory crowning his head with laurels and four slaves chained to the pedestal which support the statue.[309] The sides of the pedestal are crowded with basso relievos equally beautiful and ostentatious. The inscriptions are in Latin by Sanreuil, the most bombast nonsense that ever disgraced poetry.

The Place of Louis le Grand, or la Place de Vendome, was erected in 1699 to the glory of the same monarch. This square, or rather circle, is magnificent. The houses are regular and adorned with Corinthian pillars and much ornament. In the centre is an equestrian statue of Louis XIV on which the words "Victori perpetuo" are modestly engraved.[310]

The place of Louis XV was erected in the year 1763. The statue is by Bouchardon, a name in great repute in France. If his fame depends on this work the French must be blind or infinitely good-natured for it is most miserably executed. The King is dressed in a Roman garb and the pedestal is supported by the four cardinal virtues, which give rise to the following pasquinade—

> Bouchardon est un animal
> Et son Ouvrage fait pitie;
> Il met le vice à cheval
> Et quatre vertus à pié.[311]

The statue fronts the gardens of the Tuileries; on one side is the river Seine, on the other a very magnificent façade in imitation of the front of the Louvre. It is ornamented with colonnades, pillars of the Corinthian order, statues, trophies &c. but it is at present a mere wall, there being no buildings behind this superb front.[312]

I believe nothing remains to be mentioned but the three Theatres, the most magnificent of which is the opera in the palace of the Tuileries; the stage is more spacious than ours; the scenes are admirably painted and are let down from above, not shifted in our manner. The orchestra consists of fifty musicians and I have seen in the grand choruses one hundred and fifty persons on the stage. They generally act what they call *Fragments* which are a strange medly of dancing and singing with detached parts from different stories. I confess they infinitely exceed us both in dancing and singing as well as in the dress of the actors and scenery of the house. Vestris, Dauberval and

Mademoiselle Allar are the best dancers.[313] Mr Le Gros and Madam Rosalè are the first singers. Madam Arnould has the greatest merit as an actress, tho' Duplon is great in tragedy, especially in Medea.[314]

This house, like the other theatres, is long and badly illuminated by which means you cannot distinguish the company in the back boxes.

The French Comedy is the least distinguished of the three, which shews the vitious taste of the people, since nothing is acted there but French plays and those of the best authors; neither are the actors deficient, considering the little encouragement they meet with.[315] Privelle is admirable in low-life; he may justly be called the French Shuter.[316] Old Bonnval is a good comedian. Delonville is held in the greatest repute as an actor but he has a monotony is his voice which is extremely unpleasing.

The Italian Comedy is much frequented.[317] No regular plays are acted there but little musical entertainments, like the Padlock, or Maid of the Mill. When this company was first licensed they were to act in *Italian* only that they might not interfere with the French Comedy. But by degrees they have introduced these *petits pieces*, with speaking Harlequins who now and then speak French and often Italian by way of keeping within the line of their original institution. Nothing can be more absurd than introducing a dialogue on the stage in two different languages; one speaks in French, the other answers in Italian. The harlequin, tho' fifty years of age and corpulent, is very active and said to be the best in the world.[318] La Ruette and his wife are both excellent; the man as an actor, the wife both as actor and singer.[319] Madam Trial's beauty and voice are beyond anything I have ever seen or heard; add to this that she acts with much propriety and great spirits.[320]

The Pit or Parterre as it is called is an inclined plain without a bench which is always full of poor, well-dressed people. I say *poor* because nothing but poverty could induce a man to stand for a whole evening wedged in such a place.

You are never interrupted with riots or disturbances as in England, for sentinels with their bayonets fixed stand in different parts of the theatre who on the least tumult drag out the delinquent, be he whom he may, and carry him before a magistrate.

I had almost forgot to mention the King's Cabinet of Natural Curiosities in the Rue St Victoire, which on account of the greatness as well as the rareness of the collection, is well worthy notice.[321] It consists of various rooms full of minerals, fossils and petrefactions; of all kinds of wood in small polished pieces; of precious stones, birds, fishes, beasts and insects, arranged with the utmost regularity. Among many curious things which I do not recollect having seen before were the bark of an American fern tree which is almost black and looks like small shells stuck close together; the wolf's eye, a stone as black as jet and resembling in shape the eye of a wolf; the amiantes, a stone with which thread is made and some sea cabbage petrefied white.[322]

An uproar in the street has called me to my window, which is of too ludicrous a nature to be omitted. A taylor and the porter of the opposite house were the disputants. The taylor was *linguâ melior* but blows succeeded words and victory was declaring for the porter when the taylor fell but rose like another Antaeus from the earth with double vigour, having armed his right hand with a stone which in an instant dislodged two of the porter's teeth and concluded the combat as I must my letter, assuring you that I am, my worthy friend,[323]

ever yours

Letter XVII

Paris, Sept. 15

Dear Sir,

Supposing you to be tolerably well acquainted with Paris, I must now take you to the places in the neighbourhood; but you must first enter into a contract with the man you hire your carriage of, to keep it for a month. That contract you must take with you; the expence of it is six livres,* a mere form which does not bind you to keep the coach for a month but it is done to avoid the imposition you otherwise will be subject to of paying six livres every time you go out of Paris in your carriage. Having obtained your contract and hired your coach I would advise you of a Sunday evening to drive to St Cloud, which is two short leagues from Paris. I prefer Sunday, the gardens being open on that day to all ranks of people and the peasants of the neighbourhood and the Burgeois of Paris who dance in all parts of the gardens, tend greatly to enliven the scene.

In your way to St Cloud you go thro' the village of Passi, delightfully situated on the edge of a hill, washed by the Seine, almost opposite to the Champ de Mars. From this little town you have a good view of Paris. At a small distance is a hunting-box of the king's, called La Muette, situated at the entrance to the Bois de Boulogne.[324] You will not ill spend half an hour in walking round the gardens. The avenues are very pleasing; one is terminated by the Chateau of Madrid built by Francis I and is the model of the palace in which he was confined in Spain and was so called to satisfy the conscience of the King who, upon oath, promised Charles V that he would return to Madrid if he did not ratify the treaty.[325]

---

* In other words, pay six livres to the King's coach office for a permit to go out of Paris in your own carriage which will stand good for a twelve-month but you must always have it with you.

In your road from La Muette you must pass through the Bois de Boulogne, a royal forest full of game and divided with avenues for the convenience of pursuing it. Almost a mile beyond this wood is the village of St Cloud, situated upon the river Seine, six miles west of Paris. In the church is preserved the heart of Henry III who was basely murdered by Jacques Clement, a fryar of the Dominican order in 1589. Henry III succeeded his brother Charles IX who was brother to Francis II. In Henry ended the line of Valois after a reign of fifteen years in civil war with the Hugonots under the king of Navarre and with the league under the Duke of Guise and his brother the Duke of Mayenne.[326] By virtue of the Salique Law, the Crown descended to Henry IV, King of Navarre, the elder branch of the family of Bourbon, descended from Robert Count of Clermont, second son of Louis IX who, from the piety of his life and innocence of his manners, was called St Louis. He died in 1270 and left two sons with issue, Philip the Hardy of the house of Valois and Robert Count of Clermont of the house of Bourbon. The posterity of Philip reigned three hundred and nineteen years. After the reign of thirteen kings the Crown evolved by inheritance to Louis XII who was succeeded by his son Francis I and from him the Crown devolved to his son Henry II, the father of Francis II, Charles IX and Henry III.

The Palace of St Cloud belongs to the Duke of Orleans, is situated on the declivity of a mountain, washed by the Seine; on the right are the gardens, on the left the town.[327] The view from the house is delightful—the Seine meandering thro' the vale which you catch in many different points of view. You look over the Bois de Boulogne, which is a beautiful wood, and the city of Paris terminates the prospect. On Sundays and festivals the house is open to all the world; the rooms consequently are dirty and the little furniture you see far from elegant. The gallery is a marble apartment and the statues and paintings in it are well preserved. The paintings are chiefly by Mignard.[328]

The gardens are laid out with much art. The river Seine forms a fine canal at the extremity of the gardens, on the edge of which is a terrace planted with rows of trees. The whole is ornamented with statues, groves, vistas and cascades. There is one jet d'eau which throws up the water eighty feet. This is in a little bottom surrounded with lofty trees and the water playing about the tops of them has a very pretty effect.

In these gardens are temporary stalls for the sale of ribands, toys, cakes, fruit &c. with moveable pamphlet shops where (this being a privileged place) you may buy books which are either from their immorality or irreligion prohibited elsewhere.[329]

The grand entrance to the Palace from the situation of the hill is obliged to be oblique which takes off from the magnificence. This is indeed a defect which could not easily be obviated but I have never seen a place in France without some glaring absurdity. Here you see a palace which speaks the magnificence of a prince and a little bason of water in the great court not large enough for a duck to swim in.

Your next trip may be to St Denis which is six miles from Paris on a level pavement with a mall on each side shaded with a double row of trees. The road is so straight that you can see from one end of the avenue to the other. St Denis church terminates the view one way, the Fauxbourgs of Paris the other. The church and the Benedictine convent are the only things worthy your attention. The church was begun by King Pepin and has been much altered and enlarged by successive monarchs which give a patch-work appearance to the outside. The gates are of brass, embellished with figures and much admired for their antiquity. The windows are painted which give a gloomy solemnity to this mansion of kings. The nave is a much admired piece of Gothic architecture. I cannot say that I saw anything either curious or magnificent in the tombs. Some had nothing but antiquity to recommend them, others were remarkable only for the greatness of the names they were intended to perpetuate, among which was the monument of Marshall Turenne with Charity pouring money from an urn.[330]

The church of the Benedictines is a modern edifice of free-stone and is one of the grandest I have seen. The gardens are extensive with shady walks and pleasing prospects. The treasures of the Abbey, if the jewels are not fictitious, must be immense, exclusive of saints' bones, apostles' fingers, pieces of the real cross and such like trumpery which superstition would purchase at a very high rate. There are some antiques which merit the greatest attention; especially the bust of Tiberius on an onyx, half as large again as a crown piece. The laurel wreath is of the finest auburne, the other parts of the stone as white as snow. Likewise a piece of rock chrystal, in an oval shape, seven inches by four, on which is engraved our Saviour upon the cross, with Mary Magdalene and the other Mary on their knees. This is set in gold and adorned with jewels. But the greatest curiosity is an oriental agate made into a cup which contains above a pint. It has two handles which are part of the same stone. The bacchanals are represented on the outside in basso relievo, executed with a degree of boldness to be equalled only by the ancients; many parts of the figures stand out free from the side of the vase. It is supposed to be two thousand years old and to have belonged to Ptolemy Philadelphus.[331]

You must now proceed with me to Versailles, four leagues distant from Paris, built by Louis XIV, with more expence than judgement, on an artificial eminence in a swampy valley. You arrive at it by a grand avenue of four rows of trees, the middle walk of which is fifty yards wide. At the end of this avenue, on the right and left are the stables, in form of a crescent, most magnificently built, fronting the palace at the distance of a quarter of a mile. There are stables for five hundred horses but the inside is dark and gloomy and the stalls are divided only by a bail, which is hung too low to be useful and gives a mean appearance to the whole.[332] The horses as well for the field as for draught are chiefly English.

From thence you come to the Parade well lined with the Dutch and Swiss guards. You then enter the first court and, by an easy ascent proceed to a smaller, thro' which you pass on to a third which is paved with black and white marble, having a fountain and a marble bason in the center.[333] On each side of these courts are grand pavilions falling back like the garden front of New College in Oxford but with a greater number of wings.[334] The top of the chapel appears above the other buildings which destroys the uniformity of the view and some parts of the walls are built of brick, which is disgusting to the eye, and diminishes the grandeur of this amazing pile of building.

The front towards the gardens is wonderfully magnificent, adorned with trophies, busts, statues and all the ornaments which sculpture could devise. Its whole extent is six hundred yards; in the center of the building is a grand portico a hundred yards in length, supported by marble pillars of exquisite workmanship.

You enter the apartments by a marble staircase, ten yards wide which is as dirty as an alehouse kitchen and, what is very extraordinary, on the landing place are two or three little stalls where snuff-boxes and toys are publickly sold. Having escaped the civility and importunity of these pedling merchants, you pass thro' a suite of rooms where are the soldiers and officers of the guard, into the grand gallery called Le Brun's gallery from having painted on the ceiling the most memorable actions of Louis XIV from the Pyrenean* treaty to the peace of Nimeguen.†[335] It is seventy-two yards in length with seventeen windows fronting the gardens, the same number of looking glasses on the other side correspond with the windows. The interstices are filled with statues,

---

*   The peace of the Pyrenees was conducted between France and Spain in 1659, during the protectorship of Richard Cromwell.
†   The grand contracting powers at Nimeguen in 1677 were Louis XIV, Charles II and King William, then Prince of Orange. Spain and Sweden had plenipotentiaries there, but were not principals to the treaty.

some of which are real antiques; of these Diana and Germanicus are the most striking.

The Chapel would be as elegant as superb were it not that the windows are plain glass, the outer edges excepted which are most tawdrily bedecked with yellow flower de luces.

There is an infinite number of pictures by the best hands but the apartments are in general so gloomy that you see them with little satisfaction. The family of Darius at Alexander's feast by Le Brun is in the marble saloon, at the end of which is painted the Apotheosis of Hercules by Le Moine in which piece are a hundred and forty figures.[336]

St Michael and the Devil by Raphael. St Sebastian by Vandyke. Hercules on the funeral pyre, Hercules fighting the Hydra and the centaur and Dejanira by Guido. These were the pictures which most pleased me. In the Hall of Venus is an antique statue of Cincinnatus which ought to be studied, the better to judge of the great inferiority of the moderns.

Some part of the furniture is amazingly rich; as gold candlesticks, a chandelier of rock chrystal which can be penetrated only by a diamond, and a golden clock of curious mechanism; before it strikes the hour two cocks clap their wings and crow, two folding doors fly open and the statue of Louis XIV comes forward, an angel descends and crowns him, the clock strikes, the angel retires in a flying attitude, the king withdraws, the doors close and the show is over. All these figures are of solid gold and the statue of the king is a model of his statue in the Place des Victoires with the viro immortali on the pedestal and the conquered kingdoms chained beneath his feet.[337]

The apartments are dirty which cannot be wondered at when you are told that all the world rove about the palace at pleasure. I went from room to room as my choice directed me, into the king's bed-chamber, dressing room &c in all of which were numbers of people (and many but indifferently clad). But these are the little privileges for which the people have bartered their liberties and I doubt not but an order to prohibit any one's entering the palace, as is the case at Buckingham House, would raise as great a tumult among them as with us the annihilating of the trial by jury or any other great constitutional law.

Having stayed in the palace as long as you please, you may walk into the gardens with as little molestation where you will find as much to admire, there is such a profusion of water, statues, water-works and marble that the eye is sated with magnificence. Opposite to the center of the palace is a canal of sixteen hundred yards long, on which are many pleasure boats. In another point of view you see the orangery which covers at least one acre of ground, the trees large and full of fruit, planted in tubs which, when the severe weather comes on, are removed into vaults designed for that purpose.

As you stand above the orangery you will be struck with a most beautiful amphitheatre, formed by trees rising one above the other, beyond which is a spacious piece of water. All the steps, nay the basons and edges of the canals and reservoirs are entirely of marble. Statues in every part of astonishing beauty but all the male statues are mutilated by express order of the late Queen; they, like our first parents, were naked and not ashamed but the Queen, having tasted of the tree of knowledge, ordered the statues to be unmanned and the defect to be concealed with fig-leaves.[338]

The most beautiful statues are opposite to the front of the house, beyond the first bason. Castor and Pollux; Milo of Crotona with one hand in the cleft of a tree while a lion is fastening on his buttocks but in this is a palpable defect: his legs are very properly set against the root of the tree, his knees straightened, his body leaning back, as endeavouring to extract his hand the arm of which, by a strange oversight, is in a bent position.[339]

Perseus delivering Andromeda;[340] a dying Gladiator supporting himself with one hand on the ground, the other elbow leaning on his thigh, with drops of blood issuing from his side. This, in my opinion, the first figure in the gardens. An Appollo Belvidere, a dying Cleopatra and the Rape of Proserpine enclosed with arcades of marble which is called the colonnade. The baths of Appollo are most justly admired where Louis XIV is represented under the character of Appollo attended by his six favourite mistresses.[341] On each side is a group consisting of a man preventing a horse from drinking in the bason below: the thirst of the horse is most naturally expressed, his knees bent, his head and neck extended, his nose pushed forwards, as endeavouring to suck up the water which he cannot reach.

In one part of the gardens is a thick labyrinth in which are interspersed the fables of Aesop, cast in lead, which are contrived to spout out water in a thousand different shapes.

The two Kellers, Marsi, Bernini, Girardon, Tuby and Domenic Gendi executed the chief of the figures for the water-works. The bason of Neptune is infinitely superior in magnificence to the other water-works. It is on the right-hand of the garden front.

There is a jet d'eau that rises seventy-eight feet which spouts out of the mouth of Enceladus oppressed by the weight of a mountain.[342]

At the extremity of the gardens, on the right of the grand canal is the beautiful little palace of the Trianon built in the Italian taste, only one story high but entirely of marble. The front extends a hundred and twenty yards and the wings are joined by a colonnade formed of twenty-two marble pillars, adorned with sculpture and the entablature is embellished with statues. There are few things within the house which merit particular observation. They shew you a porphyry table, said to be the best in Europe. There is likewise a good map of France described on a table by being inlaid with different coloured marbles and another marble table on which is a butterfly inlaid so naturally and the colours so rich that it requires a nice eye to avoid being deceived.

There are two excellent pictures: the one of the Count of Thoulouse, bastard of Louis XIV, in the character of a sleeping cupid, by Mignard;[343] the other is St Louis kneeling by Coypel.

If I had not just seen the gardens of Versailles I should have admired the water-works and statues here; notwithstanding which I cannot help being struck with the Laocoön and his sons, a noble group copied from the antiques by Tuby.

Within a stone's throw of this palace the king is now building another called the Little Trianon, neither so elegant nor magnificent but it seems to be the foible of the present monarch to waste his treasures on his mistresses and buildings, tho' he is too old for the one and has no taste for the other.[344]

It is a pleasant walk of three short miles from Trianon to Marli in which you will probably see more game than you ever saw in England.[345] Just within the gardens is the house of the Swiss, where you may get a good dinner and tolerable wine which, if you please, they will serve up in any part of the gardens.

The house was built by Louis XIV after the design of the celebrated Mansart. The situation is in the bosom of a vale; on each side are six pavilions of two rooms each, almost hid by the trees. These are destined for the reception of the princes of the blood and the grand officers of state during the King's residence here which is generally for six weeks in the year. The octagon hall is the only room in the house that looks princely, tho' the whole is built in an admirable taste.[346]

There are some fine pictures by Vandermeulen, representing the sieges of Mastricht, Cambray &c.[347] The other pictures have no great merit but the history of Don Quixote in the Gobelin tapestry exceeds most pictures as well in the justness of the figures as liveliness of the colours. The face of the fat Cook in the red night-cap, laughing at Don Quixote for breaking the puppets and the archness of Sancho's appearance when laughing at Mambrino's helmet are inimitable, as is the tail of a peacock over Madam Adelaide's apartment.[348]

The gardens are enchanting; the scenes picturesque, the water-works magnificent, the statues in general excellent but two or three which surpass description: the Venus de Medicis with Cupid astride a Dolphin, near the house of the Swiss at the end of the avenue; behind the second pavilion on the left of the house is a group of two Children and Goat worth coming from England to see. One boy is represented sitting on the goat and holding him by the horn with a laughing countenance while the other, all attention is cramming a cluster of grapes into the mouth of the goat who seems pleased with the deliciousness of the fruit but angry at the rough manner in which it is given.

Near this is the celebrated statue of Venus aux belles Fesses. She is looking over her shoulder at her buttocks which are uncovered; such grace, such symmetry and elegant proportions could only live in the sculptor's imagination for neither woman nor goddess was ever so admirably formed. The drapery is equally to be admired.[349]

Both the palaces of Marli and Versailles are furnished with water by a vast machine fixed on a branch of the Seine about mid-way between Marli and St Germains. Just above Marli is a large reservoir with an acqueduct between six and seven hundred yards in length, built of freestone and supported by arcades: from hence the water is conveyed in large iron pipes of about fourteen inches diameter to the reservoir at Versailles.[350]

It will be worth the trouble to walk down to the river and trace the pipes to their source. The Chevallier de Ville was the inventor. The first expense must have been enormous. The repairs are said to amount to twenty-five thousand pounds a year; I verily believe that Mr Brindley would for that sum contract to convey the water to those palaces; we are so infinitely superior in the mechanical arts.[351] This machine raises six hundred cubical inches of water to the height of three hundred and sixty feet. As I am not an adept in drawing and as it is almost impossible to make you comprehend it without a plate of it your curiosity must remain unsatisfied till I have the pleasure of explaining it in person.

It is not above two miles from thence to the palace of St Germains which is situated on a mountain twelve miles distant from Paris.[352] Had Louis XIV expended half the treasure in erecting a palace there which he did at Versailles it must have been superior to anything in Europe. There is a lofty mountain at St Germains washed by the river Seine looking over a delightful country to Paris. Mount Calvary and St Denis and a vast reach of the river are comprehended in one view.[353] A forest of six thousand acres adjoins to the palace and a grand terrace of three thousand paces, which overlooks the whole country. This is the situation of St Germains which Louis XIV had not sense enough to admire but preferred Versailles which was so boggy that he was obliged to make a hill to build on, which has no prospect of two miles extent and which has all the inconveniences of a low and damp situation, at the same time that the water is obliged to be brought from six miles distance.[354]

Having seen the prospect you have seen everything at St Germains except a picture by Poussin and St Louis giving alms by Le Brun which are in the chapel.[355] In the sacristy are two most admirable pieces, the one of the Virgin Mary feeding the infant Jesus; St John lying on his hands and knees blowing up with his mouth the fire of the chafing dish on which stands the pap-pan: this is by Michael Angelo.[356] The other is by Carracci, of the Virgin holding a dead Christ in her arms with her head bending over his face in a most moving and expressive attitude.

The palace is an old brick quadrangle, very narrow, flanked with four large towers and surrounded with a dry ditch. It was built by Francis I and is now inhabited by different families, chiefly English, descended from those, who by more than human weakness, abandoned their fortunes and their country with their ideot King, who had neither the policy to keep, nor courage to defend that crown which by inheritance descended to him.[357]

Chateauneuf is a little place built by Louis XIV at the distance of two or three hundred paces, as little worth seeing as the palace.

The last of the King's palaces that I shall recommend to you to see is Choisy; a neat little hunting box about six miles from Paris, situated on the banks of the Seine.[358] The gardens are agreeable, not magnificent; the apartments convenient but neither rich nor elegant. There is one dining room in which no servants are admitted to attend, the table being so contrived as to render their presence unnecessary. When the first course is over the King stamps his foot, the table disappears and another immediately rises thro' the floor covered with dishes. There are four dumb waiters loaded with wines on each of which is a piece of paper and a pencil to write for what is wanted; a signal is given, the dumb waiter descends and again makes its appearance with the article required.[359]

On the road we met the King's attendants who told us he was to shoot there that day. We waited till he came, which was about noon in a coach with four of his nobles. He has a manly countenance, a penetrating eye and fine features, rather corpulent and so helpless that matter of state in being assisted to get out of his carriage and upon his horse was in fact, I believe, a matter of necessity.

His dress was a green waistcoat with sleeves, a large gold laced hat and his own hair tyed negligently together. He was attended by about two hundred horsemen and forty or fifty chasseurs on foot with guns in their hands. The Prince de Soubise and the Count de March, son of the Prince de Conti, were the only nobles permitted to shoot; they fired on horseback.[360] In less than two minutes after the King had left the highway I saw hares and partridges out of number.

The moment the King had fired another gun was put into his hand, which was instantly discharged. I had the curiosity to observe his first thirty shots in which number he missed only twice. He is proud of being esteemed the best shot in the kingdom; a most royal accomplishment! Nature certainly intended him for a gamekeeper but, as a satire on mankind, let him be a King.

He constantly goes to Mass at eleven o'clock and, as constantly, hunts or shoots from that time till five in the evening. The remainder of the day is spent at table and in gaming with his nobility till his favourite sultana seduces him to her bed. This is the life of the sovereign of a great people who has acquired the title of Louis *the well-beloved.*

I knew not whether most to pity or despise his noble attendants in the field who were not permitted to partake of the diversion tho' obliged, I suppose, to offer up incense to their master's darling folly. Laudare parati si bene ructavit, si rectum minxit.[361]

Adieu!

17 Sept.
Paris

Letter XVIII

Dear Sir,

I believe I told you in my last that I threatened leaving my friends for two or three days and intended an excursion to Rouen in Normandy, being sick of Paris and its pleasures but, as I could not meet with any of my countrymen who wanted half a chaise and an *agreeable companion*, I was determined to try the humours of a French stage-coach.[362] I took a place therefore in the Rouen stage which inns in the Rue Pavée pres les Grands-Augustins. To the price I have no objection it being only half a Guinea, tho' I was not quite so well satisfied as to the time, it being two days and a half going ninety miles.

Our company consisted of two reformed Benedictines, an officer of invalids, two curés, a fat old woman, a lively widow with an Italian physician and his daughter. You will perhaps wonder how so large a pay could be accommodated. In respect of myself, as I had taken the second place, I ousted a Benedictine who had seated himself in a very snug corner to shew him that, tho' a stranger, I knew the customs and, tho' an Englishman, had sense enough to chuse a good place for myself. Stagecoach law differs in France for you chuse your place in the coach by seniority for which you refer to the book-keeper who tells you which name is first entered.

This thing which they call a coach, is of a circular form with room for ten persons if well packed together. Both before and behind are two immense baskets covered with sail cloth for the carriage of parcels that the Tout ensemble appears like a coach between two tilted wagons. It is drawn with eight horses, attended by a coachman and a postilion, both on foot. They travel at the rate of three miles an hour: the coachman is arbitrary as his monarch and we the poor passengers were obliged to be as abject as his subjects. I got out at St

Germains, with the Italian doctor as we were not afraid of the coach driving away from us, we lounged a foot for eight or ten miles.[363] In the evening we arrived at Mante which is ten leagues from Paris, tho' we were in the coach at four in the morning.[364] The zeal of the Benedictines made my first day's journey rather unpleasant. They were proselyte-mad and were extremely earnest in their endeavours to save me from damnation. They would make me dispute however unwilling I appeared to enter the lists. I told them it was not my profession neither had it been my study, that I was talking in a language of which I knew but little and in a country where I did not wish to give offence. They said it was only by way of conversation and, after having battled over most of the sacraments, they asked me if I believed in transubstantiation; I answered that I could not believe that our Saviour had eaten his own body at the last supper and that his disciples had made a meal on the master of the feast.[365] Their answer was that I wanted faith. "Voila la Raison," added one, with all the arrogance of triumph. My patience was exhausted with so much bigotry and insufferable ignorance; "Gentlemen, my hat (which I happened to be twirling on my finger) speaks French extremely well." A stare of surprise was the consequence of the assertion which immediately gave way to a contemptuous smile. "Gentlemen you don't believe me, you want faith: Voila la Raison!" It was conclusive for they ceased all further impertinence and were very civil during the remainder of the journey.

I slept at Mante in a four bedded room with my two Benedictines and my old invalid Captain. The devotion of my fellow disputants was extremely troublesome as they kept walking up and down the room for an hour repeating pater-nosters and ave-marias as hastily as a child repeats the alphabet and seemingly with as much attention.

The Farmer-general has an elegant house about two leagues from Mante on the banks of the Seine but the situation is too low to be comfortable in the Winter or wholesome at any time.[366]

Six leagues from Mante is the little town of Gaillon where is a magnificent Chateau built by Cardinal Amboise, Archbishop of Rouen.[367] The palace is annexed to the Archbishoprick and, in point of situation (being on a hill which commands the Seine and an extensive country) as well as grandeur of the building, is esteemed among the first seats in France.

We slept last night at Vaudreuil; remarkable only for a house belonging to Mr Partail, President of the parliament of Paris.[368] When compared to a great man's seat in England it has no superior merit but it is otherwise here where you can scarce see aught but Chateaus in ruins.[369]

We rose this morning at two o'clock, that we might get into Rouen (at the distance only of fifteen miles) before the heat came on which had been intolerable for the last two days. We got there to breakfast and I am so thoroughly surfeited with a stage that nothing shall tempt me to enter one again.

I have been walking the whole day and so much fatigued that I know not whether I shall be able to give you a tolerable account of this the third city of France. It is the capital of Normandy, situated on the Seine twenty-nine leagues from Paris and twelve from Dieppe. The inhabitants are very industrious and are computed at sixty thousand. The form of the town is almost a square, containing thirty-seven parishes and forty convents. The streets are infamously narrow and the houses irregular and vilely built.

The cathedral is a noble remnant of Gothic magnificence. The form of the spire resembles a card house.[370] It is covered with lead and has a most striking effect. Here is George Amboise's bell which is ten feet in diameter and weighs thirty-six thousand pounds.[371] The grand altar is under two twisted pillars, gilt surrounded with clouds and angels. Brazen gates ornamented with well executed statues enclose the upper part of the choir.

St Maclou and St Ouen are venerable Gothic churches. The first is noted for its beautiful gates which time had much impaired; the other for the strong and lively colours of the windows but especially for the tower which is deemed most beautiful.[372]

The greatest curiosity of the city is the Bridge of boats, two hundred and seventy yards long, paved with stones, which rises and falls with the tide. It was contrived by Nicholas Bourgeois, an Augustinian fryar. The boats are placed a broadside of each other, with an axle at each end which runs in a groove made in an immense pile which is driven into the bed of the river. By these means the boats have only a perpendicular motion and, each boat having a separate pavement solves the difficulty which staggers belief at the first mention.[373]

I strolled into the Marché aux Veaux, to see the Statue of Joan of Arc who was there barbarously burnt to death by the English for no other crime than endeavouring to save her country. I know not whether the credulity of the French or the cruelty of the English is most a matter of astonishment.

When I was speaking of the bridge, I forgot to mention a most delightful walk on the other side of it, a mile in extent on the banks of the Seine, shaded with leafy trees with views of the hills which encircle the place and, on your return, you see the city of Rouen with masts of vessels, peeping up, as it were, in the town, for, by taking out one of the boats of the bridge, which is done with little trouble, the ships sail through and moor close to the backs of the houses.[374]

I shall leave the place tomorrow morning and, as I intend riding post, hope to sup with my friends at Paris in the evening, tho' the distance is almost ninety miles.

Adieu!

Rouen, 20 Sept.

Letter XIX

Dear Sir,

The day before I left Paris I was fully employed in hiring a coach for which I gave six guineas to Mr Paschall, in obtaining an order from the Post-Master general to be furnished on the road with six horses, in getting a passport from our Ambassador[375] to return without molestation, and in obtaining another passport signed by the King Of France and counter-signed by the Duke of Choiseul,[376] to permit a poor Englishman to return to his country after having spent all the money he had brought with him.

On Sunday the twenty-fourth we bid adieu to Paris, pass'd thro' St Denis, which I have already mentioned to you, made a short stay at Esouen which, in point of situation, is a lovely place. It is built on a hill which commands the whole country towards Chantilly with the Seine running on one side, the Oise on the other. The Constable Montmorenci, who was disgraced by Francis I, built a castle there, which now belongs to the Prince of Condé. [377] There are three stories of the Doric, Ionic and Attic orders well preserved. The castle is square with pavilions and turrets at each angle.

From thence we went to Chantilly, another palace belonging to the Prince of Condé and Duke of Bourbon alternatively. The Castle is triangular; within, a spacious court; without, a large moat which surrounds it.[378] The approach is over a drawbridge and it is defended by cannon.

The apartments are small and the communications from one room to another are infamously awkward. The billiard and musick rooms are fitted up in the richest manner. The floors are of marble, the ceilings painted and gilt. The gallery is ornamented with the battles of Louis XIII and XIV but it is too narrow for its length. There is in this room a marble table of inimitable workmanship inlaid with different coloured marbles and describing the siege of Barcelona as accurately as if done by the brush of a painter.[379]

The Cabinet of Curiosities is superior to any private collection I have seen. The cabinet of natural philosophy is particularly rich in minerals and fossils. Titian and Paul Veronese are the only names of note in the collection of pictures which is unequal to a prince whose domains are one hundred miles in circumference.

The gardens are full of orange trees, jet d'eaus and water-works. The Park is diversified with water, bridges, wildernesses, statues, temples and, in short, everything that expence can imagine; notwithstanding which I am so partial to Stow gardens[380] that I cannot but give them the preference; at Chantilly, nature is lost in art; at Stow, art has ever nature in her view.[381]

The Menagerie is very extensive but ill stocked; the walls are covered with green lattice work between which all kinds of flowers are occasionally interwoven so as entirely to conceal the wall. This was a refinement in elegant expence which I had not the least idea of.

The Stables are more magnificent than a palace. They form a quadrangle built of the finest stone, one side is a stable containing two hundred and forty English horses. In the center of it there are statues of two horses in marble, vomiting water into a large cistern. The prince often drives thro' the stables in his carriage when he comes to view his stud.

The Manage is equally grand. It forms a rotund of prodigious extent but is left open to the sky.[382]

There was an infinite variety of carriages for state, convenience and the chase. Among the latter I must mention one of a construction most whimsically odd. It was made like a chair with a head to it but on each shaft was a seat resembling the back of a horse, terminating with a horse's head. Five persons can sit astride on each shaft, one behind the other. In this manner I saw the Prince of Condé, the Dukes of Orleans and Chartres, with two others of the nobility, go to the chase.

From Chantilly we went to Clermont where we slept. This is a small town in the Isle of France, situated on a hill, the little river de Breche runs at the foot of it. The Duke of Fitz-James has a chateau there, built in the Gothic style but much out of repair.[383] The situation is low and damp; the environs are gloomy, consisting of straight walks thro' thick groves with plenty of water, not advantageously disposed.

We left Clermont at six in the morning, breakfasted at Breteuil, a little dirty insignificant town, dined at Amiens, which is the capital of Picardy, about mid-way between Paris and Calais, situated on the river Somme, three branches of which run thro' the town. The streets are regular, the houses tolerably well built and the people, who are computed to be thirty-five thousand, wore a face of industry not often to be seen in inland towns in France.

There are some noble walks adjoining the city, and the grand mall is deemed inferior only to the mall of Tours. The Cathedral of Notre Dame was built by the English and remains a noble monument of British magnificence.[384] The nave of the church is a finished piece of architecture, two hundred and thirteen feet in length and equally admired for its proportion. The present bishop and one of the canons of the church have expended above four thousand pounds sterling in ornamenting the grand altar.[385] It represents heaven opened, with the clouds and angels, partly in painting and partly in basso relievo. On one side of the altar is St John, on the other the Virgin Mary in stone, as large as the life. On the altar are seven candlesticks of massive silver. In the choir are four cedar pillars thirty feet high, carved in the most curious manner. The filigree is so slight as to appear unable to support its own weight and what is still more extraordinary they are four single trees without a nail or a drop of glue.

The church is rich in curiosities and precious relicks. Among the former are the head of St John in pure gold which was regarded as nothing in comparison with a relick which was deemed invaluable, I mean the identical finger of the unbelieving Thomas which pierced our Saviour's side. I confess I was weak enough to prefer the mammon of unrighteousness to the finger of the apostle, especially as the golden head was ornamented with an infinite number of jewels, the offerings of the weak and the wicked who hoped to bribe heaven with trash they could no longer enjoy.

Having satisfied our curiosity and appetites, we proceeded on our journey thro' Pequigny, a small town built on a hill and watered by the Somme. From the church you have an extensive view of the country and, at about five miles distance, you see a Benedictine convent called Du-Garde, built on the edge of the river which has a very magnificent appearance.[386]

In the evening we arrived at Abbeville, the capital of Ponthieu in the province of Picardy, situated only fourteen miles from the English channel. The town is low and the country around marshy. It is divided by the river Somme, is called the *maiden* town because it never has been taken which is to me a matter of wonder as it is in the neighbourhood of Cressy and must have followed the fate of that battle had Edward thought it worthy of his attention.[387]

We breakfasted this morning at Montreuil which is most agreeably situated on a circular hill, surrounded with a wall and fosse. The vale below is watered by the river Canche. This town was taken by the Duke of Marlborough.[388]

We next passed Samers, a dirty little town with nothing in it to be observed but a Benedictine convent reputed rich. We dined at Boulogne the capital of the Boulonnais, the see of a bishop whose revenue is near a thousand pounds a year; it is divided into the upper and lower town.

The Upper Town is pleasantly situated on an eminence, commands the whole country and has a distinct view of the English coast. The Lower Town is built on the side of a hill and runs down to the river Liane, at the mouth of which is a dangerous harbour.

This town is exempted from the gabelle on salt, a most oppressive tax; from whence arose this indulgence I could not learn.[389] About midway between Boulogne and Calais we passed Wissand, called by Caesar Iccius Portus, from whence he embarked for Britain.

At length we are arrived at Calais and bless ourselves that the journey is over. From Chantilly the road has been in every respect disagreeable, up hill and down; in many places dirty, in others ill-paved—the whole country open, scarce a hedge to be seen, no carriages on the road, no appearance of traffick, no gentlemen's seats; few towns, and but now and then a straggling village swarming with beggars; a dreary prospect indeed, where every object betrayed the strongest symptoms of poverty and distress.

Calais is only eight leagues from Dover and thirty-two posts from Paris, situated in the county of Artois and generality of Amiens. I confess my surprise to see a place which has been so often mentioned in history, which withstood the army of Edward III for near twelve months and which made so considerable a figure in the treaty of Chateau Cambresis in 1559, so contemptible as it at present appears.[390] Its situation at that period was deemed so strong and its fortifications so impregnable that for the space of two hundred and ten years no monarch of France had been daring enough to attack it, from the time of Edward III till the enterprising valour of the Duke of Guise in 1558 compelled Lord Wentworth to surrender.

The town is small, the streets are narrow and the fortifications trifling. There is indeed a fossé which can be filled either with salt or fresh water and a citadel advantageously situated to annoy the enemy from every quarter. I was not allowed to enter it but it seemed incapable of making any material defence.

The barracks built by Louis XIV can accommodate twelve hundred men. The outside of the windows are surrounded with tenterhooks many of which were loaded with sheep's hinges and other offal for the use of the soldiery. I knew not what most to admire, their food or their larders.

The church, dedicated to the Invocation of the Virgin, is built in form of a cross and ornamented with eleven chapels. The grand altar is decorated with two basso relievos in alabaster; the one represents the Manna showered from Heaven; the other, the Lord's Supper. Both of them are well executed.[391]

I have just seen the captain of the Packet who comforts me by saying the wind is in our teeth and that we cannot get out of the harbour till it changes. If we are weather-bound here tomorrow I will dedicate it to the request you made me in your last by giving you some account of the manners and custom of the people but, should the wind prove fair, we shall early in the morning take leave of this nation of levity and good humour which I shall most gladly exchange for the more solid understanding and rational manners of my own country.

Adieu!

Tuesday evening
27 Sept. Calais

Letter XX

Dear Sir,

I have hitherto troubled you with descriptions of towns and palaces which every sixpenny pamphlet on the subject would probably have given you a juster idea of. As you paid me the compliment to think otherwise I submitted but you request at present a much more arduous task. Long usage and much observation are requisite to speak with tolerable precision on the manners and customs of a people. Though I have been twice in France yet my residence there has been so short that I could scarce learn the language, you therefore must expect no observations from me but such as were so striking that even inattention could not fail to remark.

I believe the climate of France to be the most healthy, the soil the most fruitful and the face of the country the most pleasing in the universe and, I hope, for the honour of human nature, that its inhabitants are the vainest and most illiterate. Can you believe that this all-sufficient people, who look on the rest of Europe with contempt, are in most of the mechanic arts at least a century behind the *savage* English as they affect to term us? In their tapestry, looking-glasses and coach-varnish they are, confessedly, our superiors but their carriages are more clumsy than our dung-carts; their inns inferior to an English ale-house; their floors, both above and below, of brick or a kind of plaister, without carpets; their joists unceiled, the windows without pullies drawn up to a certain height where they catch a hook which prevents their falling; the tables consist of three or four planks nailed together and the houses are totally destitute of every kind of elegance, I had almost said convenience. I do not mean to include the houses of the opulent great as money will purchase the elegant superfluities of every country. But in this situation you will find the inns and the houses of the gentry and tradesmen. Their gardens are most uniformly dull but in these they condescend to follow those standards of taste the Dutch. Sandy walks at parallel lines between yew hedges, parterres tortured into form and surrounded with the lively box, and trees planted at equal distances will give you a just idea of a French garden. I ought to have added that they blend the utile dulci,[392] for I remember the parterres in the gardens of the bishop and intendant of Anjou were prettily diversified with garlick, onions and other useful vegetables.[393] They are such slaves to fashion that they have eight different seasons in the year for dress which they carry to such excess of folly that they descend even to the minutiae of a ruffle and a man's character would be ruined were not the lace of his ruffles adapted to the season of the year.

Their conversation consists in compliments and observations on the weather. No flattery is too gross for them either to offer or receive. They will talk for ever but never pay the least attention to what you say. The barber and the looking-glass employ their whole time within doors and walking in a sandy mall is all their entertainment without. One of these things, the moment it enters the room, pays its respect to the glass and views the pretty fellow with wonderful satisfaction. His hat, if a thing of six inches in circumference deserves the name, is always carried in his hand, but in this the French are humble imitators of their tutelar St Denis, who has refined upon politeness by carrying, instead of a hat, his head in his hand, at least he is thus portrayed in all the statues I have seen of him.*[394]

Nothing is more common than to see gentlemen ornamented with ear-rings, while their shirts are sacking and their heads a dunghill.

In some instances they are as neat as filthy in others. At table you have a clean napkin and clean plates but your knife is never changed nor wiped. A common bourgeois will not drink out of the same cup with you, though a nobleman will spit over your room with the greatest unconcern. I have seen a

---

*   Voltaire, in a note in his *Pucelle d'Orleans* says "L'Abbé Hildouin fut le premier que écrivit, qui cet Evêque ayant été décapité porta sa tête entre ses bras de Paris, jusqu'a l'Abbaye qui porte son nom: on érigea ensuite des croix dans tous les endroits on ce saint s'était arrêté en chemin. Le Cardinal Polignac content cette histoire à une marquise et ajoutant que Denis n'avait eu de peine à porter sa tête que jusqu'a à la premier station; cette dame lui repondit; *Je le crois bien, il n'y a dans de telles affaires qui le premier pas qui côute.*"

lady, through excess of delicacy, hide her mouth whilst she used a tooth-pick and, to preserve the character entire, she has the next moment scratched her head with the sharp pointed knife she was eating with.

Ladies of fashion alone have the privilege of making themselves horrible, which they most effectively do, by applying a large patch of rouge or vermilion under each eye; the shape and colour at the discretion of the wearer. The only pretty women I have seen are among the trading people who are not allowed to disfigure themselves, neither are they obliged to be in the sun, which makes the peasants an antidote to the loosest libertine. I ought to tell you that all ranks of women, to convince you that they have neither feeling nor common sense, never wear a hat. It may be extraordinary, but not less true, for a hat they never wear. They seem as regardless of their heels as their heads, for slippers without quarters[395] are the general wear; notwithstanding which, it is amazing how well they dance and how firm they walk. I do not include the peasants: they, poor devils, have no stockings and wear large wooden shoes, lined sometimes with a piece of sheepskin to prevent galling the instep but that is a piece of luxury you seldom meet with.

In every branch of agriculture the farmers are incredibly deficient but can it be wondered at when you consider that there are no inducements for improvement. The nobility and clergy are exempted from the land-tax, a heavy assessment which consequently must fall on the occupier.[396] The gabel on salt is likewise extremely burthensome for every family is obliged to buy annually in the proportion of two bushels and a half to ten persons which, if not consumed within the year must not be sold. Add to this that the Seignior or lord (for all lands are held by vassalage) exacts *ad arbitrium* from his tenants. To what purpose then are improvements, when the King or the Lord will reap all the fruit of the farmer's industry or labour? Hence arises that misery so conspicuous in every farm. I have often seen a half-starved cow and an ass ploughing in the same yoke and I have heard it asserted as a fact that a pig and an ass are sometimes ploughing together but I can scarce believe that two such opinionated animals could be induced to work together with any degree of society. In some of the provinces the little farmers who have no barns, and can afford to build none, are obliged to thrash out the grain in the field where it grows to their great loss in the best of weather; in a wet season, to their utter ruin. For want of money to purchase waggons, they are obliged to carry both their corn and their hay on the backs of their cattle and it is with much ingenuity they will load a horse till you will see only his head and feet; at a distance he appears a moving haycock. These are the unavoidable consequences of poverty; some other instances seem the result of ignorance. For example, the cattle draw entirely with their horns; a board of two inches wide is fixed on their horns and a cord is tied to each end which is fastened to the cart. That is their method of drawing. A more uncouth method could not have been followed in the days of King Pepin.[397]

They wash their linen in a river by dipping it into the running stream, then placing it on a block or stone and beating it with a board like a battledoor. Such proofs of ignorance would surpass belief did not the notoriety of them exact your credit. Even in Paris I have seen men hold a saw between their legs and rub a stick of wood against it till it was sawed asunder.

In the whole of the city of Paris there is not a flat stone to walk on, nor a post to guard you from the carriages which are so numerous and the streets so narrow that the foot passengers are never out of danger.[398]

The lamps hang in the center of the streets on cords which are fixed to the opposite houses. If the cord breaks the lamp is destroyed as well as the unfortunate person who is passing under at the time. To light a lamp is two men's business. The one lowers it, while the other lights it which forms a temporary barrier across the streets, a method as awkward as inconvenient. Two men likewise are required to shoe a poor little bidet[399] one smith holds the horse's hoof, while the other drives the nail.

The police of France so much admired by travellers is in many instances wonderfully deficient. The whole kingdom swarms with beggars, an evidence of poverty as well as defect in the laws. This observation was confirmed at every inn I came to by crowds of wretches whose appearance spake their misery. I have often passed from the inn door to my chaise through a file of twenty or thirty of them. Even the churches are infested with them and I have seen many a devotee, in the midst of their devotions, interrupted by their importunity.

Duelling it is said is punished with death; true—if two persons (I will not say gentlemen for every rascal wears a sword and knows the use of it) fight in a house, or meet by appointment, the survivor must be hanged, for the King solemnly swears at his coronation not to pardon such offenders. But every duel is construed a rencontre; that is the parties meet by accident and then the murderer escapes unpunished, the dead being always in the wrong, the survivor pleading that he killed his adversary in his own defence. The regiment of Carabineers, when quartered at Angers, in the space of four years gave upwards of a hundred instances of what I have advanced. The civil magistrates were silent; their officers rather countenanced the practice. Add to this, a custom truly diabolical, if a gentleman strikes another, his sword alone is not sufficient atonement; nothing but death can expiate the offence.

From an ill-timed parsimony in the laws murder frequently escapes justice for the relations of the deceased must be at the expence of apprehending and prosecuting the criminal. If a man of rank commits murder, his greatness will be his safeguard and he may almost depend upon pardon.

If you are robbed on the highway you lose both your money and your life; but this seldom happens as there is in every large town a maréchaussée[400] established, which is a horse patrol of six or eight persons whose sole employ is to patrol the roads and protect the traveller. The roads are excellent and untaxed with turnpikes but these the poor peasants are obliged to make and to repair by the sweat of their brow without even the prospect of advantage accruing to them for their labour.

Their religion seems calculated for the vulgar. It consists of trumpery-saints and tinsel-ornaments; in prayers estimated by their number more than for the devotion with which they are offered. The Virgin Mary is adored with all the superstition of idolatry, while the Saviour of mankind is almost unnoticed, unless by being gibbeted in every public road, a profanation equally impious and absurd. The priests hurry over the service, which is in Latin lest it should be understood by the congregation, in the most slovenly manner; they are illiterate to a degree of contempt. The clergy are in general unacquainted with the Greek characters and most who profess a knowledge of the Latin tongue are strangers to the elegance of the language. Indeed I think illiterature seems to be the national misfortune; the infinite number of notaries in Paris will justify my observation.

When I was at Angers[401] there were in that city four thousand religious of both sexes who had dedicated their lives to idleness under the different shapes of Nuns, Mendicants and Benedictins, and who were prohibited what the deity had himself enjoined: "Increase and multiply". What immense numbers then must there be in the whole kingdom, who are restrained population, in which consists the great riches as well as power of a state. If the passions cannot be subdued what scenes of iniquity must follow! The nuns drink a liquor called volet which freezes the blood and quells those desires which might otherwise intrude on female minds, but I fear they are often obliged to call in the ecclesiastical power to their aid, and find a pampered friar to be more efficacious than rivers of volet.

All ranks of people celebrate Sunday in merriment and dissipation and it is the genteel day for routs and the play-house. Their festivals are out of number which are commemorated by idleness and pageantry, making no difference

between the feast of God's heart or the commemoration of Parson Berenger*
and celebrating with equal magnificence the Virgin Mary and the whore of
Orleans.[402]

The good qualities of the French are confined in very narrow compass.
They are lively, temperate, sober and good-humoured but in general are strangers to the manly virtues though I know two or three individuals who are not
only an honour to their country but an ornament to human nature.

Adieu!

Hotel d'Angleterre
Calais
28th Sept

---

*   On the 18th of June an annual festival is held at Angers to commemorate the abjuration
    of Berenger, Arch-deacon of Angers who had been guilty of writing against the real pres-
    ence. It draws the whole province together. The procession, when I was there, consisted
    of upwards of four thousand people who walked at noon-day with torches in their hands,
    preceded by many groups of waxen images, representing various parts of the Old and New
    Testament, dressed à la mode in laced coats, negligees &c.

The Coins of Holland

The doit is a copper coin, the size of a farthing but of only half the value.

Eight doits make a stiver, which is of a base metal, larger than a silver penny, and rather more in value. On one side is the bundle of arrows emblematic of the union of the Seven Provinces; on the reverse, is the name of the respective province in which it was coined.

Two stivers make a dubliky which is of base metal, and of the size of an English sixpence.

The sestehalf goes for five stivers and a half, is as thin as a sixpence, but in size equal to a shilling. When the bundle of arrows in form of a star, is stamped on a sestehalf, it increases its value to six stivers. On one side is a champion on horseback; on the reverse the arms of the province.

The goode skelling is likewise worth six stivers, and differs from the sestehalf only in the size, being broader.

The gilder or florin is twenty stivers, of tolerable silver, and almost as large as our half-crown. On one side is the figure of a man à l'antique, leaning upon the bible with his left hand, holding a spear in his right.* On the exergue are these words "Hâc nitimur, hanc tuemur". Had the words been reversed, the motto would have applied; at present they stand as proof of Dutch stupidity.

---

* I am inclined to think that this device was taken from John Boccold, or Beukels, a journey-man taylor of Leyden who was an Anabaptist prophet, and in the year 1534 became king of Munster. This John of Leyden carried a bible in one hand and spear in the other; and coined money stamped with his own image.
  [Editor's note—The man 'à l'antique' is in fact 'de Nederlandse Maagd'—the Dutch Maiden. In her right hand is a staff on which is the Cap of Liberty and her left hand rests on the Bible or book of Law. The words 'HANC TUEMUR'— 'this we protect'—occurs next to the staff whilst HAC NITIMUR—'on this we depend'—is next to the Bible.]

The ducat is a gold coin, worth five gilders and five stivers, about the size of a half guinea. It is said to be the purest gold of any European coin. On one side is a warrior armed cap-à-pié with a sword in one hand, the bundle of arrows in the other. On the exergue, Concordiâ res parvae crescunt; on the reverse, Mo.ord. Provin. Foeder. Belg. ad leg. imp.*

A ryder is a gold coin, rather thicker than the ducat, value seven florins. On one side is an equestrian figure of a warrior, completely armed, in the act of attacking sword-in-hand; on the reverse a lion rampant, with a sword in one paw, the bundle of arrows in the other: it is marked 7 G^l.

The gilder, the ducat and the ryder are most beautiful coins.

Table of Dutch Coin

Dutch	English
A doit	half a farthing
A stiver	one penny
A dubliky	two pence
A sestehalf	five pence halfpenny
A goode skelling	six pence
A gilder or florin	twenty pence
A ducat	9 shill. and 6 pence
A ryder	12 shill. and 9 pence

This calculation is not perfectly exact; for a shilling goes only for eleven stivers; half a crown for twenty-eight; and a guinea for eleven gilders eleven stivers; but you will seldom be allowed more than eleven gilders eight stivers for a guinea.

A stiver's intrinsic value is something more than an English penny, otherwise we should lose one shilling and nine pence in the exchange, as there are in eleven gilders, eleven stivers only two hundred and thirty-one stivers, which valued as pence, amount to no more than nineteen shillings and three pence.

---

*   Concordiâ res parvae crescunt = Through Concord little things grow; MOneta ORDinarum PROVINciarum FOEDERatorum BELGicarum ad LEGem IMPerii = Coin of the government of the provincial confederation of the Belgians conforming to imperial law. [Ed.]

Guineas are current in all parts of Holland and if you can carry over new guineas, it will be to your advantage, as at Helveot and Amsterdam you will get the full change of eleven gilders eleven stivers.

The Flemish Coin

The smallest piece of currency is a liard, of the size and value of an English farthing.

The demi-sous answers to our half-penny both in size and value.

The ten-liard piece is a base silver coin of the size of a sixpence; on one side a cross, on the other the imperial arms, worth two-pence halfpenny English.

A placart is half a schelling, or three sous and a half, larger than a sixpence, bearing a cross on one side and a spread eagle on the other.

A five sous piece is as large as our shilling; on one side a cross, on the other the imperial arms.

A schelling is of the same size, but better metal, worth seven sous; on one side the arms of the Empress, on the other a lion rampant holding a sword in one paw, sustaining a shield with the other.

There are two-schelling pieces, which differ from the schelling only in size.

The demi-couronne is the size of an English half-crown, and is worth four schellings and a placart; on one side a cross, on the other a spread eagle, with the imperial arms in the middle.

The couronne is the size and value of an English crown.

Four couronnes nine sous, or thirty-seven schellings two sous, are change for an English guinea.

The Flemands compute by florins, which are not real coin as in Holland, but imaginary like our pound Sterling. For instance thirteen florins one sous make a guinea.

The ideal florin answers to twenty sous by which means you get nine sous in the change for every guinea.

For a Dutch ducat you have in change seventeen schellings one sous which is equal to ten shillings in English.

Their silver money is so basely adulterated that it will not pass out of the territories of the Empress.

There is a gold coin called an imperial; but I never met with one.

The Coin of France

Three deniers make one liard; four of which, one sol or halfpenny English; twenty sold one livre, which like our pound Sterling is imaginary; but by that the French always compute.

Twenty-four livres make one louis d'or.

A denier is an ancient copper coin, not so large as Charles the IId's farthing.

A two-liard piece is in size between a farthing and a halfpenny; in value equal only to a farthing.

A sol is somewhat larger.

A six-liard piece is of thin copper, the size of an English sixpence, slightly washed with silver and is marked thus LL.

The two-sols piece differs only from the six-liard piece in thickness, and by being stamped with a single L:—The thickness is the safer distinction, as the impression of the letters are often worn out.

The six-sols piece is of the size and value of our silver threepence.

The douze-sols piece answers to our sixpence.

The vingt-quatre sol is like an English shilling, both in size and value.

The half-crown is three livres.

The crown-piece six livres; four of which make a louis d'or, which is about the size and value of a guinea.

The coin of the reigning King is the only current coin in France; which in the gold and silver is most minutely observed; but their copper is so adulterated, that the stamp is little regarded.

You must also compute either by sols or livres; generally by sols till you arrive at five livres: you therefore say a thing cost quatre-vingt or cent sols.

A franc and a livre are synonymous for the same specific sum, yet are distinguished in their application. In small numbers you use the word franc, as six francs; but when you come to computations above a hundred, you adopt the word livre.

Distances and Cost of Travel

The manner and expense of travelling
from London to Helveot

In a chaise and four, with post-horse for the servant	£ 6 – 10 – 0

At Harwich

The agent's permit	£0 – 13 – 6
Porters for trunks, at 6d each	0 – 0 – 6
To the officers of the customs	0 – 1 – 0
To the boat to the vessel	0 – 1 – 0
Bed in the cabin	1 – 1 – 0
Cabin-boy	0 – 1 – 0
Porter at Helveot	0 – 1 – 0
The fees and passage for one person are	1 – 19 – 0

The seventy-two mile stone is in the middle of the town of Harwich, yet by inn-keepers computation you are obliged to pay for seventy-four miles.

There is a coach goes from the Spread-Eagle in Gracechurch-street: fare, 12s.

The rout and distance from place to place

From London to

White Hart		Rumford	12
Red Lion	12	Ingolstone	24
Blue Potts	14	Witham	38
Three Cups	14	Colchester	52
White Hart	10	Manningtree	62
White Hart	12	Harwich	74

From Harwich to Helveot 36 leagues.

The manner and expense of travelling for three gentlemen and one servant from Helveot to Utrecht

	Gilder	Stiver	Doit
For ringing the bell at Helveot	0	5	4
For a stage-waggon to the Brill	3	17	0
To the waggoner	0	5	4
For the ferry to Boar's island	0	12	0
Post-waggon over the island	0	16	0
Ferry to Maeslandsluice	0	5	0
Roof of the Treckschuyte to Delft	1	4	0
Ditto to Rotterdam	1	12	0
Ditto to Delft	1	12	0
Ditto to the Hague	0	18	0
Ditto to Leyden	1	10	0
Ditto to Harlem	3	0	0
Ditto to Amsterdam	2	1	0
To Utrecht without the roof	3	4	0
	21	1	8

We travelled one hundred and thirteen miles for about £1 – 19s – 6d English. A stiver for the boy who rides the horse for the boat is a handsome gratuity.

The rout and distances from Helveot to Utrecht

			Miles
Sun	to	The Brill	7
Blackmoor's Head	5	Maeslandsluice	12
Stadt's Doele	8	Delft	20
Swine's Hoof	10	Rotterdam	30
Le Parlement d'Angleterre	15	The Hague	45
Golden Ball	12	Leyden	57
Golden Fleece	16	Harlem	73
The Star in the Ness	10	Amsterdam	83
Chateau d'Anvers	30	Utrecht	113

The manner and expense of travelling from Utrecht to Lille

	Gil.	Stiv.	Doit.
A coach and four from Utrecht to Breda	54	0	0
Ditto to Bergen-op-Zoom	21	0	0
Ditto to Antwerp	22	0	0
A coach and pair to Brussels	16	0	0
Ditto to Ghent	15	0	0
The barge to Bruges	4	0	0
Coach and pair to Courtray	14	0	0
Ditto to Lille	8	0	0
The permit at Menin to enter France	1	8	0
	155	8	0

Or about £14, 4s. English

Four places in the Diligence from	*Liv.*		
Lille to Paris at 55 liv. Each	220	0	0
To the coachman 3 liv. Each	12	0	0
Baggage at 3 sous per pound	35	0	0
	262	0	0

Or £11, 9s English.

N.B. Provisions and lodgings are included in the fare.

The rout and distance from Utrecht to Lisle

	To Golcombe	—	18
To Prince Cardinal —	24 Breda	—	42
	15 Rosandale	—	57
La Cour d'Holland —	6 Bergen-op-Zoom	—	63
Le Grand Laboureur —	21 Antwerp	—	84
La Grüe —	12 Mechlin	—	96
L'Hotel Imperial —	12 Brussels	—	108
	15 Alost	—	123
St Sebastian —	15 Ghent	—	138
Le Fleur de Blé —	24 Bruges	—	162
Le Chatelet —	24 Courtray	—	186
L'Aigle étendu —	6 Menin	—	192
L'Hotel Royal —	9 Lisle	—	201

From Lisle

To Douay	—	21
15 Cambray	—	36
24 Peronne	—	60
66 Senlis	—	126
30 Paris	—	156

The manner and expence of travelling from Paris to Calais

	Liv.
To Mr. Paschal-Sellier près la monnoye, for the hire of a coach to Calais	144
For six horses at 7 livres 10 sous per post for thirty-two posts and a post-royal	247
To two postilions 2 livres per post	64
	455

Or about £20 Sterling.

Fifteen sous per post is sufficient to give a postilion: None but the English give so much.

Remember when you hire a chaise to agree with the master, that he shall be at the expence of all repairs that may be necessary on the road; otherwise you will be accommodated with a crazy vehicle, that it may be repaired at your expence. The proper method is to get an order from the owner on the person you are to deliver the carriage to, that he should reimburse you the expence of the repairs.

The rout and distance from Paris

		To St Denis	6
A la Poste	—	21 Chantilly	27
A Cynge Blanc	—	15 Clermont	42
Les Bons Enfans	—	48 Amiens	90
		9 Pequigney	99
L' Etoile de Jour	—	21 Abbeville	120
La Cour de France	—	30 Montreuil	150
Leon d'Or	—	24 Boulogne	174
Hotel d'Angleterre	—	21 Calais	195

A post-royal is a shameful imposition to plunder travellers: For at going in and out of Paris, Versailles, Lions or any other place where the King keeps his court, the first post, though in fact but two leagues, demands a double price; and from the King residing there is called royal.

The French compute distance by leagues or by posts but never by miles.

A post is two leagues, which I believe is not more than five English miles.

It costs about 5d. English per mile to ride post; the same for a person in a two-wheeled chaise with two horses; but the hire of the carriage is not included in that expence.

By the ordonnance of 1757, every person à franc etrier shall pay twenty-five sous per post for his own bidet, the same for his guide's.[403]

For a carriage with two wheels and two horses, one person only being in it, two livres ten sous must be paid per post.

If there are three horses, or two persons in the chaise, or a servant behind it, three livres sixteen sous must be paid a post.

A four-wheeled chaise with four horses shall pay five livres.

The post-masters may refuse to carry the baggage exceeding one hundred weight behind and forty pounds before the carriage.

Expence of travelling from Calais to London

For half the pacquet	2	12	6
To the sailors	0	10	6
Boat to land us*	1	1	0
Porters	0	5	0
Chaise and four, and post-horse for the servant	7	4	0
From Calais to London	11	13	0

Rout and distance from Calais to London

Ship		To Dover —	24
Red Lion	—	16 Canterbury —	40
George	—	16 Sitingborne —	56
King's Head	—	11 Rochester —	67
Marquis of Granby	—	15 Dartford —	82
		15 London —	97

a This expence was occasioned by the time of the tide and roughness of the weather, which prevented the vessel coming into the harbour: Boats therefore came off for us, and took advantage of our sickness and impatience, by extorting two guineas for putting eight of us on shore at the distance of half a mile.

	Manner of travelling	Expence £	s.	Miles
From London to Harwich	Post-chaise and four	6	10	74
Harwich to Helveot	In the pacquet	8	0	118
Helveot to Utrecht which includes the tour of Holland	In treckschuyte	2	0	113
Utrecht to Antwerp Which includes Dutch Brabant	In a coach and four	8	16	84
Antwerp to Lisle which includes the Austrian Netherlands	In a coach and pair	5	7	115
Lisle to Paris	In the Diligence	11	9	156
Paris to Calais	In a coach and six	20	0	192
Calais to Dover	In the pacquet	4	9	24
Dover to London	In a chaise and four	7	4	75

Number of miles in the whole tour is nine hundred and fifty-one.

The conveyance of three gentlemen and one servant amounts to £73 – 10s:— Absent from England nine weeks, three of which spent in Paris.

Bibliography

Alcouffe, D. *et al., Le trésor de Saint-Denis,* (1991).

Anon., *A Description of Holland: or the Present State of the United Provinces,* (1743).

Avery, C., *Giambologna: the Complete Sculpture,* (1987).

Black, J., *The Grand Tour in the Eighteenth Century,* (1992).

Boswell, J. in Pottle F.A. (ed.), *Boswell in Holland, 1763-64,* (1952).

Bott, E., *The Excursion to Holland and the German Spa 1767* quoted by Strien, G.D. van, *Tourism and Casual Travelling* in Moll, T. van, *Expanding Horizons: Travel and Exchanging Ideas through the Ages,* Journal of the XIIIth annual ISHA Conference, Nijmegen, (2002).

Browne, E., *An Account of Several Travels through a Great Part of Germany,* (1688).

Churchill, C., *The Traveller's Complete Guide through Belgium, Holland and Germany,* (1815).

Clifford, D., *A History of Garden Design,* (1966).

Cole, W. in F.G. Stokes (ed.), *A Journal of my Journey to Paris in the Year 1765,* (1931).

Defoe, D., *A Tour Through the Whole Island of Great Britain* (P. Rogers [ed.], London, 1971).

Descamps, J.B., *Voyage Pittoresque de la Flandre et du Brabant,* (1769).

Dibdin, T.F., *Biographical, Antiquarian and picturesque Tour of France and Germany,* (1821).

Essex, J., in W. Fawcett, (ed.), *Journey of a Tour through part of Flanders and France in August 1773,* (1888).

Gallet, M & Bottineau, Y., *Les Gabriel,* (1982).

Garrioch, D. *The Making of Revolutionary Paris,* (2004).

Gemmett, R.J.,(ed), *Dreams, Waking Thoughts, and Incidents: In a Series of Letters from Various Parts of Europe,* (1971).

Geyl, P. *The Revolt of the Netherlands, 1555-1604,* (1932).

Gray, T., in Beresford .J (ed.), *Letters of Thomas Gray,* (1925).

Halbertsma, R.B., *Scholars, Travellers and Trade: the pioneer years of the National Museum of Antiquities in Leiden 1818-1840 ,* London, (2003).

Hammersley, V., *Letters from Madame de Sévigné,* (1955).

Hargreaves-Mawdsley, W.N., (ed.), *Woodforde at Oxford, 1759-1776,* (1968).

Hilton, D., *Kings, Queens, Bones and Bastards,* (1998).

Israel, J.I., *The Dutch Republic: its Rise, Greatness, and Fall—1477-1806,* (1995).

Jardine, L., *The Awful End of Prince William the Silent*, (2005).

Jones, C., *Paris: Biography of a City*, (2004) .

Levi, A., *Louis XIV*, (2004).

Licquet, T., *Rouen—its History and Monuments: a Guide to Strangers*, (1840).

Lister, M., *A Journey to Paris in the Year 1697*, (1967).

Loveday, J. in Markham, S. (ed.), *John Loveday of Caversham 1711–1789*, (1984).

McCann, T.J., *Sussex Cricket in the Eighteenth Century* (2004).

McManners, J., *French Ecclesiastical Society under the Ancien Régime: a Study of Angers*, (1960).

McManners, J., *Church and Society in Eighteenth Century France, Vol. 1*, (1998).

McManners, J., *Church and Society in Eighteenth Century France, Vol. 2.* (1999)

Marchand, J., (ed.), *A Frenchman in England 1784*, (1933).

Marshall, J., *Travels through Holland, Flanders, Germany*, (1772).

Mérot, A., *French Painting in the Seventeenth century*, (1995).

Moore, J., *A View of Society and Manners in France, Switzerland and Germany, Vol. 1*, (1779).

Motley, J., *The Rise of the Dutch Republic*, (1901).

Namier, L. & Brooke, J., *The House of Commons 1754-1790, Vol. 1 Introductory Survey, Constituencies, Appendices*, (1968).

Nicolson, B., *Joseph Wright of Derby: Painter of Light, Vol. 1*, (1968).

Norton, L. (ed.), *Saint-Simon at Versailles*, (1959).

Nugent, T., *The Grand Tour*, (1756).

Oppenheimer, P., *Rubens: a Portrait*, (1999).

Schama, S., *The Embarrassment of Riches*, (1987).

Scott, J., *Paris Revisited in 1815 by way of Brussels*, (1816).

Shennan, J.H., *The Parlement of Paris*, (1968).

Smollett, T., *The Adventures of Peregrine Pickle*, (1751).

Smollett, T., *Travels in France and Italy*, (1766).

Southey, R., in J. Simmons (ed.), *Letters from England*, (1951).

Sterne, L., *Life and Opinions of Tristram Shandy* in *The Works of Sterne*, Vol. 1, (1900).

Temple, W., *Observations upon the United Provinces of the Netherlands*, (1672).

Thrale, H. in Tyson, M. & Guppy, H. (eds.), *The French Journals of Mrs Thrale & Dr Johnson*, (1932).

Uglow, J., *The Lunar Men: the friends who made the future*, (2002).

Wiebenson, D., *The Two Domes of the Halle au Blé in Paris*, The Art Bulletin, Vol. 55 No. 2 (1973).

Winstanley, R.L. (ed.), *The Diary of James Woodforde, Vol. 1*, (1996).

Winstanley, R.L. (ed.), *The Diary of James Woodforde, Vol. 2*, (1997).

Winstanley, R.L. (ed.), *The Oxford and Somerset Diary of James Woodforde, 1774–1774*, (1989).

Winstanley, R.L. (ed.), *The Diary of James Woodforde, Vol. 10—1782–1784*, (1998).

Young, A. in Maxwell C. (ed.), *Travels in France during the years 1787, 1788 & 1789*, (1950).

Notes

Notes to Introduction

1 Southey, R., *Letters from England*, ed. J. Simmons (1951).
2 Bott, E. *The Excursion to Holland and the German Spa 1767*.
3 Pallant House, built 1712/13, is now a much-admired art gallery. Harry was left a moiety of the manor and lands of Middleton [-on-Sea] in 'Lisbon' Peckham's will—Victoria County History, *A History of the County of Sussex, Vol. 5, pt. 1*.
4 Mundy was granted an M.A. degree 'by honour' on 21 May 1761—R.L. Winstanley (ed.) *The Diary of James Woodforde, Vol. 2—1763–1765* (1997)— entry for 21 May 1761. The quotations from Woodforde's diary come from the definitive edition published by The Parson Woodforde Society. The portraits of the Markeaton Hunt (sometimes called the Derby Hunt) were painted *c.*1763—B. Nicolson—*Joseph Wright of Derby: Painter of Light, Vol. 1* (1968).
5 Benedict Nicolson, author of the Wright *catalogue raisonné*, draws attention to a note in Wright's MS Account Book which reads—'The letter in Mr Mundy's Picture to be dated from Amberley in Sussex. It may conclude with "Your friend Harry Peckham" not Henry'. Nicolson suggests that this may be a note for another portrait of Mundy, now lost—B. Nicolson (1968) *op.cit.* Amberley was Peckham's home.
6 On the night of his graduation Mundy and his friends were described by a fellow collegian as 'all as drunk as Pipers'—Winstanley—*ibid*—21 May 1761.
7 Jenny Uglow, *The Lunar Men: the friends who made the future* (2002).
8 National Archives, PROB 11/1152.
9 Court of Chancery: Six Clerks Office Pleadings W1806 C5J—Crawford v Rous.
10 Winstanley, R.L. (ed.) *The Diary of James Woodforde, Vol. 1—1759–1762* (1996)—entry for 6 October 1759. A selection, edited in 5 volumes by John Beresford and entitled *The Diary of a Country Parson* was published 1924–31. The Oxford entries appear in W.N. Hargreaves-Mawdsley (ed.) *Woodforde at Oxford, 1759-1776* (1968).
11 Winstanley—*ibid*—20 December 1760.
12 Winstanley—*ibid*—12 October 1761.
13 Winstanley—*ibid*—23 July 1761.

14   Winstanley—*ibid*—4 June 1761. Peckham was a keen cricketer and was
     one of the 'Committee of Noblemen and Gentlemen of Kent, Hampshire,
     Surrey, Sussex, Middlesex and London' who on 25 February 1774 met at the
     Star and Garter, Pall Mall, London and drew up 'The New Articles of the
     Game of Cricket;' the foundation of the laws of the modern game. Mention
     is also made of him in Timothy J. McCann, *Sussex Cricket in the Eighteenth
     Century* (2004).

15   Winstanley—*ibid*—28 January 1761.

16   Winstanley—*ibid*—4 April 1762.

17   Winstanley—*ibid*—24 November 1762.

18   Winstanley, R.L. (ed.), *The Diary of James Woodforde, Vol. 2—1763–1765* (1997)
     10 March 1764.

19   Winstanley—*ibid*—1 June 1763. Woodforde had been victim of a similar
     escapade earlier in his university career when Peckham's friend Mundy
     graduated and was one of a group who broke down Woodforde's door 'all to
     shatters for Funn'—Winstanley—*ibid*—21 May 1761.

20   The first edition of the *Tour* was published in 1772 but neither in it or any
     subsequent editions is mention made of the year in which the tour was
     undertaken. The dates on the letters—'Thursday Aug. 3' etc—indicate that the
     most likely year was 1769.

21   Thomas Nugent, *The Grand Tour, Vol.1* (3rd ed. 1778).

22   John Purnell, who was Warden when Peckham first went up to New College,
     won some notoriety by refusing to condemn some undergraduates accused
     of toasting the health of King James—J.Buxton & P. Williams (eds.), *New
     College, Oxford, 1379–1979* (1979).

23   Young A. *Travels in France during the years 1787, 1788 & 1789*, ed. C. Maxwell
     (1950).

24   McCann T.J., *op.cit.*

25   Entry on Wilson in L. Namier & J. Brooke, *The House of Commons 1754–1790,
     Vol. III, Members K–Y*, (1964).

26   British Library, Add. 49607 A, Peckham (Harry), Letters to T.S. Wilson.

27   Namier & Brooke, *op.cit.*

28   There were two seats for the county. Wilson and Peachey both agreed to
     allow Lord George Henry Lennox to take one of them. Lennox received 3583
     votes, Wilson 1957 and Peachey 1855—L. Namier & J. Brooke, *The House
     of Commons 1754–1790, Vol. 1 Introductory Survey, Constituencies, Appendices*
     (1968).

29   Winstanley R.L, *The Oxford and Somerset Diary of James Woodforde, 1774–1774*
     (1989)—entry for 21 November 1775.

30   Winstanley, *Oxford and Somerset Diary of James Woodforde, 1774–1775*—entry
     for 14 December 1775.

31   De la Motte was spared the grislier aspects of the sentence but more than
     80,000 people turned out to witness his execution at Tyburn. Darnay's trial in
     Dickens' *A Tale of Two Cities* is said to be based on that of De la Motte.

32   Winstanley R.L.—*The Diary of James Woodforde, vol. 10—1782–1784*—entry for
     14 April 1784.

33   'Ostentatious Monuments…'—from Harry Peckham's will—National
     Archives PROB 11/1152.

Notes to Letter I

34 *Purpureus pannus*—a purple patch or passage of especially flamboyant writing. Used by Horace in *Ars Poetica*, 15.

35 The factual matter—value of coins, distances etc—to which Peckham here alludes is in fact confined to the appendices.

36 Peckham's anonymity was retained until after his death in 1787. The fourth edition of the *Tour*, published in the following year, revealed the author as 'the late Harry Peckham Esq. One of His Majesty's Council and Recorder of the City of Chichester'.

Notes to Letter II

37 Peckham had, presumably, not encountered—or chose to ignore—Thomas Nugent's *The Grand Tour*, a second, expanded edition of which had been published in 1756.

38 Colchester Castle is in fact built of stone and brick—much of it quarried from the Roman town. It has the largest Norman keep in Europe.

39 The tidal river is the Stour estuary.

40 Harwich had done nothing to improve its reputation since Defoe, more than forty years earlier, had described its inhabitants as "far from being famed for good usage to strangers" (D. Defoe, *A Tour Through the Whole Island of Great Britain,* P. Rogers (ed.), London, (1971)).

41 John Canton F.R.S. (1718–1772)—English physicist; elected to a fellowship of Royal Society after reading a paper on the making of artificial magnets. His work on phosphorescence was only published in 1768 (i.e. the year before Peckham undertook his tour).

42 In fact, Captain Story is more likely to have employed a half-minute log-glass; the distance between the knots bearing the same proportion to a nautical mile as half a minute does to an hour.

43 Bavins—bundles of brushwood.

Notes to Letter III

44 One stiver was the equivalent of an English penny—see Appendix A.

45 Count of Marche—William de la Marck, 'a wild, sanguinary, licentious noble, wearing his hair and beard unshorn according to ancient Batavian custom'— (John Motley, *The Rise of the Dutch Republic*, London, (1901)) was the leader of the sea-beggars who took Brill in the name of the Prince of Orange at the beginning of April 1572. Peckham's use of the word 'malcontents' is misleading; that term being more generally applied to a pro-Catholic, anti-Orange faction which emerged later in the decade.

46 Jan van Oldenbarneveldt (1547-1619)—Dutch statesman, lawyer and Grand Pensionary; negotiated the English evacuation in 1616 of the 'cautionary towns,' which they had held since 1585.

47 Aart van der Houwen points out that at this time the southern part of the Hook of Holland sandspit was joined to the island of Rozenburg and was

known as the Bear. It appears that Peckham confused the name of the sandy Hook with that of the island (personal correspondence).

48   The comparison with Thames livery barges was often made by English travellers in Holland—e.g. "The usual way of travelling in *Holland* and most parts of the United Provinces…is in the *Treck-scoots* or Draw Boats which are large covered boats not unlike the barges of the livery companies of London, drawn by a horse at the rate of three miles an hour" (Nugent).
     Not everyone enjoyed this means of transport as much as Peckham appears to have done. Six years earlier Boswell complained to his friend John Johnston of travelling between Leyden and Utrecht "nine hours in a sluggish trek schuit, without any companion, so that I brooded over my own dismal imagination" (Pottle F.A.[ed.], *Boswell in Holland 1763–1764*, 1952). Joseph Marshall, characteristically sour, complained of the vessel's master who 'will crowd it with twenty, or even twenty-five, on account of the profit of the fares; and indeed, I believe, if he could pack them as close he would stuff it as full as a barrel of herrings'— *Travels through Holland, Flanders etc…in the year 1768, 1769 and 1770* (1772).

49   Charles Campbell who, like Peckham, approved of the treckschuit, supplied some further retails of the *roef*—"there are four oblique windows, which move up and down and a table in the middle with a long draw, filled with papers. There is also a spitting box and a little iron pot containing burning turf, for accommodating the smokers with a light. The seats are covered with handsome cushions. The *roef* is generally occupied by the genteeler passengers, though the price is but about three pence an hour. So steady is the motion of the vessel that a person may read, write or even draw in it… A person may have the whole *roef* to himself by giving proper notice." (Charles Campbell, *The Traveller's Guide through Belgium, Holland & Germany*, 1815, p.17).

50   Marshall, by contrast, attributes the decline of Delftware manufacture to competition from Staffordshire cream-coloured ware which 'rivalled the delft, not only in the British consumption but even in their own city' (Marshall),

51   Nugent was of the opposite opinion of the Armamentarium—"The arsenal of the States is also worth seeing, the magazine of powder belonging to which accidentally blew up and destroyed a great part of the town in the year 1654 but it has since been rebuilt to great advantage" (Nugent).

52   10 July 1584—William I was assassinated by Balthazar Gérard, a cabinet-maker's apprentice, with a pistol bought with money given to him by his victim. The murder is the subject of Lisa Jardine's recent book *The Awful End of Prince William the Silent: the first Assassination of a Head of State with a Hand-Gun*, (2005).

53   The inscription composed by Contantijn Huyghens (1596–1687), the father of the great physicist Christiaan, concludes as follows: "Who spent his life in sincere devotion to God, Wisdom and invincible Spirit, and who did not fear Philip II, King of Spain, the terror of all Europe. And who was not defeated by him, but who deprived him of his life through a bought executioner, by vile betrayal and godless deceit." (Gout M., *Wilhemus van Nassouwe: the Mausoleum of Willem of Orange in the New Church at Delft*).

54   a)Van Tromp, Maareten Harperstszoon (1597–1653)—great Dutch admiral, he died in battle and the monument shows his head resting on a cannon, his body stretched over a ship's rudder.

b) Heyn (or Heijn), Pieter Pieterzoon (1578–1629)—Dutch naval commander, born Delfshaven. After being a Spanish galley-slave he eventually became vice-admiral of the Dutch East India Company—defeated Spanish off San Salvador and at Matanzas Bay (1628), capturing Spanish silver flotilla with value of 12 million guilders.

55 John Loveday who visited Rotterdam in 1737 was likewise impressed by the Bomb Quay—"The Bomb-key is the first part of Rotterdam, for the Merchants' houses there are very handsome; before them is a Walk half an English Mile long between Trees, the Maas with Ships on it runs by the Walk and there is a View of the Country across it." (Sarah Markham [ed.], *John Loveday of Caversham, 1711–1789,* (1984)).

56 The English Church of St Mary on the Haringfliet was consecrated in 1709, Queen Anne having given £500 towards its construction. It was demolished in 1913, the site becoming that of the Eye Hospital (Oogziekenhuis). Much of the woodwork was purchased by the English author A.C. Benson who presented it to Selwyn College, Cambridge where it forms the panelling at the west end of the Hall.

57 Erasmus, Desiderius (1466–1536), Dutch scholar and humanist. In fact he died at Basel. Of the statue, Marshall adds, 'the pedestal is of marble, inclosed with iron rails, the expression is not great' (Marshall).

58 Peckham's orientation was incorrect. Delft and The Hague are to the NW, Dordrecht to the SE, Amsterdam to NNE and Utrecht to ENE. Brielle is, however, to the W of Rotterdam.

59 The church of St Laurence (Laurens kerk), although damaged, survived the blitzkrieg of May 1940.

60 Jan van Brakel (1618–1690)—Dutch admiral, hero of the battle of the Medway (1667) when he broke the defensive chain across the river. The inscription may be translated as follows:

Sacred to the Memory and Mortal Remains
Of the unconquered hero
Jan van Brakel
Rear Admiral
Beneath this stone lies Brakel
Terror of the High Seas
To whose lot fell Fame, Iron and the Billows of the Sea
We are indeed in error if he is not now belching forth Flames
Look, at this very moment
He who broke the Iron Chains in breaking them now.

Notes to Letter IV

61 James Boswell had met and dined with 'Greffier Fagel', 14 May 1764. Henrik Fagel (1706–1790) was Secretary of State for the States General. His daughter Johanna Catharina married the brother of Boswell's literary lady-friend Belle de Zuylen—see F.A. Pottle (ed.), *Boswell in Holland, 1763–64.*

62 Aeneas's fleet was driven in a storm onto the coast of Carthage where Dido was Queen; Virgil, *Aeneid, Bk. 1.*

63 'Grove nods at grove…' from Alexander Pope's *Epistle to Burlington* in
    which he satirises the idea of uniformity and symmetry in a garden. William
    Beckford was no more impressed when he visited "the pompous parterres of
    the Greffier Fagel" in 1780, "Every flower that wealth can purchase diffuses its
    perfume on one side; whilst every stench a canal can exhale poisons the air on
    the other"—R.J. Gemmett (ed.), *Dreams, Waking Thoughts, and Incidents: In a
    Series of Letters from Various parts of Europe*, (1971).

64 By the Treaty of Ryswick, 1697, which ended the War of the League of
    Augsburg, Louis XIV gave up his conquests in Luxembourg and Lorraine, the
    Dutch were granted the right to garrison the frontier towns of the Spanish
    Netherlands and William III was recognised as King of England.

65 'The prince' was William V (1748–1806), Prince of Orange, Stadtholder of the
    United Provinces, 1751–1795.

66 The prison is the Gevangenpoort from which the arrested Grand Pensionary
    Cornelis de Witt (1623–1672) and his brother Johann were, in 1672, dragged
    by the mob and brutally murdered.

67 Since 1822 the Royal Cabinet of Paintings has been housed in the adjacent
    Mauritshuis, built in 1633–44 for Prince Johann Maurits van Nassau-Siegen.

68 *Adam and Eve in Paradise* is today believed to have been the work of both
    Peter Paul Rubens (1577–1640) and his friend Jan Brueghel (1568–1625).

69 The 'most capital painters' to whom Peckham refers include: Raphael [Raffaelo
    Sanzio] (1483–1520); Rembrandt Harmensz van Rijn (1606–1669); Van Dyck,
    Anthony (1599–1641); Holbein, Hans (1496/7–1543); Teniers, David the
    Younger (1610–1690); Wouwermans, Philip (1619–1668).

70 'cymar'= a loose, light dress or undergarment.

71 Peckham here describes Potter's most famous painting, *The Young Bull*. It
    measures 235.5 x 339cm and is signed and dated 1647. It was one of the many
    works of European art plundered by Napoleon and repatriated in 1815. Tsar
    Alexander I's offer to purchase it—for £15,000—was rejected—John Scott,
    Paris Revisited in 1815, (1816).

72 No such painting is still attributed to Leonardo.

73 Claude-Joseph Vernet (1714–1789).

74 Antoine Coypel (1661–1722).

75 Gerard Dou (1613–1675), *Young Mother with her Child*, signed and dated 1658.

76 The Binnenhof.

77 These 12 panels were, in fact, painted by Otto van Veen (1556–1629) in the
    years 1612-13 and were purchased by the States-General for their Assembly
    Chamber in the Hague. They remained at the Binnenhof until 1799. In 1808
    they were acquired by the Royal Museum, Amsterdam and are now in the
    Rijksmuseum. There is an interesting discussion of their significance in S.
    Schama, *The Embarrassment of Riches,* pp.76–79 (1987). By the time they
    were painted Hans Holbein had been dead for seventy years. 'The great Lord
    Bolingbroke' was Henry St. John, first Viscount Bolingbroke, who had been
    the chief architect of the Treaty of Utrecht of 1713.

78 The Batavians were the ancient inhabitants of the island of Betuwe, between
    the Rhine and the Waal.

79 'The House in the Wood'—Huis ten Bosch, erected in 1647. Frederick Henry
    (1584–1647) was the grandfather of William III of England and husband of
    Amalia van Solms (1602–1675).

80 *Vulcan's Forge* is in fact the work of Theodor van Thulden (1606–1669), a Flemish painter strongly influenced by Rubens.

81 Anne of Hanover (1709–1759), Princess of Orange. On her marriage the States General congratulated George II upon choosing for his daughter a home in a 'free republic such as ours!'—quoted in Jonathan I. Israel, *The Dutch Republic: its Rise, its Greatness and Fall; 1477–1806*, (1995).

82 Edward Browne's description of his visit in 1668 is similar—"The Course where the Coaches meet, the Pall-mall, the Wood, the Park, do much beautifie it, and the way from hence to *Scheveling,* from whence his Majesty returned into *England,* is very remarkable, it being a streight way cut through the Sand-hills, and paved with Brick for three miles, having on each hand four or five rows of Trees, and *Scheveling* Steeple at the end of it." *An Account of Several Travels through a Great Part of Germany* (1688).

83 Visiting the same garden in 1780 William Beckford wrote: "An Englishman ought certainly to behold it with partial eyes, since every possible attempt has been made to twist it into the taste of his country. I need not say how liberally I bestowed my encomiums on Count B's tasteful intentions; nor how happy I was, when I had duly serpentized over his garden, to find myself once more in the grand avenue."—R.J. Gemmett (ed.), (1971).

84 Possibly Captain John Albert Bentinck (1737–1775), grandson of the first earl of Portland. He had been a commander under Lord Anson at St Malo in 1758. Peckham may, however, be confused with Christian Edward Anthony Bentinck, also a British naval captain who had died in 1768. He had been a friend of James Boswell—see F.A. Pottle, *Boswell in Holland, 1763–64.*

85 Obdam, Jacob, Heer van Wassenaer—in supreme command of the Dutch fleet when his ship blew up at the Battle of Lowestoft, 3 June 1665. The memorial, by Batholomeus Eggers, consists of a square canopy on four composite columns beneath which is the statue of Van Wassenaer Obdam in armour flanked by a page carrying a helmet. The inscription describes him as another Hercules who has beaten his way through the flames to reach heaven.

Notes to Letter V

86 James Boswell's father, Lord Auchinleck, who had been a student in Leyden, had stayed '*op de hoek van de Vliet* in the street called Rapenburg'—see Pottle, *Boswell in Holland, 1763–64*, p.52.

87 'The number of students, one year with another, is seven or eight hundred in each of the universities of Leyden and Utrecht…They all live in private lodgings, except thirty or forty Poles and Hungarians, who have a college in each of the universities, where they are maintained at the public expense, which are the only enclosed foundations here'—Anon., *A Description of Holland: or the Present state of the United Provinces*, (1743).

88 Scaliger—Joseph Justus Scaliger (1540–1609): French classical scholar; Protestant, moved from Geneva to Leiden in 1593.
Leipsius—Justus Lipsius (1547–1606): classical scholar.
Salmasius—Claudius Salmasius (1588–1653): French Protestant humanist and philosopher; moved to Leiden 1631.

Boerhaave—Hermann Boerhaave (1668–1738): Dutch; professor of botany and medicine, brilliant lecturer.

89 Sensitive plant—Mimosa predica, a tropical American plant of the pea family whose leaves bend down when touched.

90 Papenbrochius—Gerard van Papenbroeck (1673–1743); he left his portrait collection to the Amsterdam Athenaeum, the forerunner of the University of Amsterdam. For the part he was to play in what eventually was to become the National Museum of Antiquities see R.B. Halbertsma, *Scholars, Travellers and Trade: the pioneer years of the National Museum of Antiquities in Leiden 1818-1840,* London, (2003).

91 The Bibliotheca Thysiana, built 1655 to house the library of Joannes Thysius (1622–1653) who left money for the building of a public library.

92 The stock of the poet Andrew Marvell (1621–1678) has perhaps risen since Peckham's day. Edmund Ludlow (1617?–1692), soldier, politician and regicide, escaped abroad at the restoration and wrote his *Memoirs.* John Loveday, visiting the town in 1737, noted of the public library that "here hang the pictures of Lipsius, Joseph Scaliger, Erpenius, D. Heinsius, Isaac Casaubon, Sir T. More, Bishop Fisher &c."—Sarah Markham (ed.) *John Loveday of Caversham 1711–1789,* (1984), p.264.

93 Now in the Municipal Museum 'De Lakenhal', Leiden. Peckham appears not to be familiar with the word triptych.

94 Antonis Mor (c.1517/20–1576/7)—much travelled painter, known in England as Sir Anthony More and in Spain as Antonio Moro.

95 (a)The Continence of Scipio was an extremely popular subject in European art. During the Second Punic War Publius Cornelius Scipio (c.235–183BC) took the Spanish city of new Carthage. Together with great quantities of booty he might have taken as a concubine the most beautiful girl in the city. Instead he returned her to her family.
    (b) The siege of Leiden was lifted on 3 October 1574. It had begun on 26 May.

96 Christian Muller's organ in the Great Church of St Bavo's has 5068 pipes and is nearly 30m high. It had been played by the 10 year old Wolfgang Amadeus Mozart just three years before.

97 Laurens, Janszoon, often called Coster (c.1370–1440)—by some credited with the discovery of printing before Gutenberg.

98 The Wouvermans brothers were painters of Haarlem, mention of which appears to have prompted Peckham's footnote.

99 Johann Fust, or Faust (1400–1466)—German printer, appears to have had no connection with Haarlem. He was a goldsmith from Mainz who made loans to Gutenberg to enable him to complete the printing of the Bible. Gutenberg was unable to re-pay the debt and Fust received the printing press in lieu and with it published the Gutenberg Bible in 1465. Fust the historical character may have been a prototype for the conjuror of legend.

100 Aldus Manutius, or Aldo Manucci (c.1450–1515)—founder of Aldine Press, produced first printed editions of many Greek and Latin classics.

101 Cornelis van Haarlem (1562–1638). 'The Feast of the Gods' is *The Marriage of Peleus and Thetis.* The foot of the lame Vulcan is in the foreground of the picture—now in the Frans Hals Museum, Haarlem. Simon Schama points out that Cornelis had been commissioned to provide paintings for the Haarlem

residence of the Prince of Orange (the Prinsenhof) and, specifically, to supply a replacement for a panel of Maarten van Heemskerck's which had been damaged by the Spanish during the siege of 1573—"This work—the *Massacre of the Innocents*—and a lascivious *Monk and Nun* (the 'Haarlem Wonder') must have been directly aimed at contemporary sensibilities."—S. Schama, *The Embarrassment of Riches,* (1987).

Edward Browne, a century earlier wrote of his visit: "In the rooms are very good Paintings by *Hemskerk,* and *Goltzius,* as his *Prometheus* and other Peeces; but *Cornelius van Haerlem* most delighted me, in his peeces of *Herods* killing the Innocent Children; his feast of the Gods, in which *Vulcans foot* is esteemed at a great rate; and another Picture of a Frier and a Nun at a Collation, not inferiour to the rest." *An Account of Several Travels through a Great Part of Germany,* (1677). At the time of Peckham's visit these pictures hung in the town hall.

102 Also hanging in the Town Hall at this time was *Mary Magdalene* by Jan van Scorel (1495–1562). Although hardly dressed 'in the style of a peasant' there is more than a hint of archness in her expression. Today it hangs, on long-term loan from the Rijksmuseum, in the Frans Hals Museum, Haarlem.

103 Haarlem was blockaded throughout the hard winter of 1572–73 by the troops of Alva's son, Don Fabrique, and did not capitulate until 12 July. The entire garrison and selected citizens were slaughtered—just over two thousand in total.

104 Nugent expressed himself in similar terms—"The public places or squares of Amsterdam are not very handsome; the principal is that which they call the *Dam* and is very irregular having no other ornament but the stadthouse or guildhall which indeed is a magnificent edifice but somewhat disfigured by an old building which stands before it where they weigh goods."—T. Nugent, *Grand Tour,* Vol. 1.

105 Jacob de Wit (1695–1754)—outstanding Dutch decorative painter. His name has entered the Dutch language to describe a kind of trompe-l'oeil imitative of marble relief.

106 Batholomeus van der Helst (1613–70)—very popular portraitist in Amsterdam in mid-seventeenth century, eclipsing Rembrandt. Reynolds (1781) wrote of his *Banquet of the Amsterdam Civic Guard in Celebration of the peace of Munster* (now in the Rijksmuseum and clearly the picture admired by Peckham), that it is "perhaps, the first picture of portraits in the world," adding that it exceeded his expectations as much as Rembrandt's *The Night Watch* fell below them.

107 In 1599 the overseers of the House of Correction had been granted a monopoly in powdered brazil wood for the dyeworks—see Schama, pp.19–20. Marshall, approvingly, points out that for the incorrigibly lazy there was in the Rasphouse an 'admirable contrivance; it is a cellar with a pump, into which they let water, so proportioned to the strength of the person that he shall be able, with infinite labour in pumping it out, to save himself from drowning.'—*Travels through Holland, Flanders, Germany…*(1772).

108 Thomas Nugent, in *The Grand Tour* Vol. 1, developed this theme—"The unhappy recluses both here and in other cities of Holland are but very few in number which makes their hardship the severer, as they have the misfortune to be singled out for so disreputable a confinement when such numbers of their fellow delinquents carry on their illicit trade with impunity…those

under whose custody they are, who look like grave and sober matrons, permit gentlemen for a trifle of money (that *Dutch* God) to have access to them, so as to speak to one another through the grates on which occasion it is customary for them to entertain their visitors with such abominable discourses and indecent actions as are shocking to men of any sense or morality."

109 *O.E.D.*—'snick or snee' obs. late 17th century: fight with knives. Nugent issued a similar warning about what he refers to as 'their music rooms'— "Those who chuse to satisfy their curiosity in this respect should take care to behave civilly and especially not to offer familiarities to any girl that is engaged with another man, otherwise the consequences might be dangerous for the Dutch are very brutish in their quarrels"—*Grand Tour*, Vol. 1.

110 The Portuguese Synagogue—the Amsterdam Esnoga—still in use today was inaugurated in 1675.

111 Sardam = Zaandam.

112 Broek in Waterland.

Notes to Letter VI

113 In later, posthumous, editions of the *Tour*, to which 'a Tour through the Northern Provinces ... by a Gentleman of Groningen' has been added, this letter is described as written 'In the Hoorn Trechsckuyte'. It is followed by an entirely new 'letter'—from Dockum in Friesland—beginning 'The reflections of my last were broken short by our stopping to change boats at Monikedam!'

114 Dort and Tergow—variant names for Dordrecht and Gouda.

115 Police—did not have current meaning until early 19th century. Peckham uses the term to mean government in the sense of public order.

116 Sir William Temple (1628–1699)—statesman and author, ambassador at The Hague, author of *Observations upon the United Provinces of the Netherlands*, (1672).

117 Oliver Goldsmith (1730–1774) had briefly studied medicine at Leiden in 1754 before travelling across the Continent to Italy. The poem was begun whilst he was still abroad but was not published until 1764.

118 Charles V had formally introduced the Inquisition into the Netherlands in 1524 and in 1550 Inquisitors became Imperial functionaries whom citizens of the Empire were bound to assist. On succeeding his father in 1556 one of Philip II's first acts had been to re-organise the episcopacy, replacing the four bishoprics of the Low Countries with a total of 18.
(a) Antoine Perrenot Granvelle (1517–82)—first minister to Margaret of Parma, Philip's governor of the Netherlands; Archbishop of Malines, created cardinal in 1561; an able politician but his policy of repressing Protestantism created such outrage that in 1564 he was forced to retire.
(b) Alva (or Alba), Ferdinand Alvarez de Toledo, Duke of (1508–1582), brilliant but brutal Spanish general, accomplished statesman. In 1567 sent by Philip II to be lieutenant-general in the Netherlands where his inner council became known as the Council of Blood.
(c) The Counts of Egmont and Horn, although moderate and conciliatory opponents of the worst excesses of Spanish rule in the Netherlands, were in

1568 suddenly seized, tried and executed, becoming martyrs to the Dutch cause.

The Union of Utrecht of 1579 brought together the six northern, Calvinist provinces, together with Gelderland, so as effectively to oppose Spain and suppress Catholicism.

119 Easterlings—traders from about the shores of the Baltic.

Notes to Letter VII

120 'Trajectum ad Rhenum' of the Romans (= ford on the Rhine). Later Oude Trecht (= old ford) from which Utrecht evolved.

121 Charles Churchill agreed—"The Mall is esteemed the principal ornament of Utrecht and is perhaps the only avenue of the sort in Europe still fit to be used for the game which gives its name to them all. The several rows of noble trees include at the side both roads and walks but the centre is laid out for the game of [pall-]mall, and, though not often used, is in perfect preservation. It is divided so as to admit two parties of players at once, and the side boards sufficiently restrain spectators." *The Traveller's Complete Guide through Belgium, Holland and Germany*, (1815). Pall-mall is a game rather like croquet played with a wooden ball struck with mallets.

122 Marshall likewise ascended the steeple of Utrecht cathedral and 'had the satisfaction of viewing over Five of the Seven provinces and a great way further towards Cleves in Germany'—*Travels through Holland, Flanders, Germany...* (1772).

123 Van Mollem's Gardens on the Vecht. He was a wealthy silk manufacturer.

124 (a) The Union of Utrecht brought together, under the Prince of Orange, the provinces of Holland, Zealand, Friesland, Utrecht and Gelderland as a rival union to that of the Walloon provinces formed at Arras a fortnight before.
(b) The Treaty of Utrecht of 1713 ended the War of the Spanish Succession. Peckham takes the Whig view of the treaty. The Tory government reached a separate, secret agreement with the French, in effect deserting her allies (including the Dutch—the origin of the expression 'Pervidious Albion') leaving them with little option but to agree to a peace. Britain, however, gained more from the treaty than Peckham allows.

125 Adriaan Florensz Dedel (1459–1523)—elected pope in 1522. Attempted to restrict the sale of indulgencies and bring about other reforms but died without achieving a great deal.

126 "Here lies Adrian VI, who esteemed nothing in his life more unhappy than that he had been called to rule."

Notes to Letter VIII

127 Golcombe = Gorinchem.

128 Occurs all over Europe—"Give of your possessions while they are yours to give. After death they are no longer yours."

129 Wimbledon Common and Blackheath were used for military reviews. George III had reviewed the Guards on Wimbledon Common in 1767.

130 Breda was not the capital of Dutch Brabant. As conquered territory the northern part of Brabant was put under the dominion of the States General of the United Provinces. This situation lasted until the French occupation at the end of the eighteenth century. In 1796 the people of Dutch Brabant created the province of North Brabant with 's-Hertogenbosch as capital: a position which was accepted by the central authorities.

131 Despite the formidable fortifications, Breda was only briefly besieged by the French in 1793 before the commandant, Alexander Van Bylandt, surrendered.

132 The present tower is only 320 ft high. Peckham would have seen the church with an 80 ft high cupola built in 1702 following a fire which destroyed an earlier wooden structure.

133 This remarkable monument to Engelbrecht II (d.1504) and his wife Cimburga Von Badenis is in the Princes' Chapel in the Grote Kerk.

134 The Castle was subsequently (1826–28) transformed into a military academy, a function which it still possesses.

Notes to Letter IX

135 Rosindale = Roosendaal.

136 The fall of Bergen in September 1747 helped bring the War of the Austrian Succession to an end. It sparked off a wave of anti-Catholic rioting across the country. The treaty of Aix-la-Chapelle was signed in the following year.

137 Cohorn = Menno van Coehoorn (1641–1704), Dutch military engineer.

138 Lowendhall = Ulrich-Frederick Waldemar, Comte de Lowendhal (1700–1755), marshall of France.

Notes to Letter X

139 Empress Queen = Maria Theresa (1717–1780), Holy Roman Empress, Queen of Hungary.

140 The building of the Citadel began in October 1567. Two thousand workmen were employed in its construction and it was completed within a few months at a cost of 1.4 million florins. It was pulled down, apart from the old medieval castle at its heart, in 1859.

141 Fall of Antwerp—captured by the French army of Maurice, Comte de Saxe (1696–1750) in February 1746 in the war of the Austrian Succession.

142 Most notoriously by mutinous Spanish troops in November 1576—the so-called 'Spanish Fury' when 6,000 citizens were killed. There was no sacking following the city's capitulation to Parma's troops in 1585 but Protestants were forced either to convert to Catholicism or leave Antwerp. Over the next four years some 38,000 people moved north—Israel, *The Dutch Republic…*, (1995).

143 William Beckford who visited Antwerp in 1780 was certainly impressed— "After crossing a broad, noble river, edged on one side by beds of osiers, beautifully green, and on the other by gates and turrets, preposterously ugly, we came through several streets of lofty houses to our inn. Its situation in the Place de Mer, a vast open space, surrounded by buildings above buildings,

and roof above roof, has something striking and singular. A tall gilt crucifix of bronze, sculptured by some famous artist adds to its splendor; and the tops of some tufted trees, seen above a line of magnificent hotels, add greatly to the effect of the perspective." Gemmett, R.J. *Dreams, Waking Thoughts…*, (1971).

144 This must have been the day of Peckham's arrival in Antwerp—16 August being St Roch's Day. St Roch was thought to offer protection against the plague.

145 *The Descent from the Cross* (1612–14), originally painted for the Altar of the Chapel of the Arquebusiers—now in the south transept. Smollett satirises such enthusiasm as Peckham's in the person of the artist Pallet in *The Adventures of Peregrine Pickle*, (1751)—"They returned to the Great Church and were entertained with the view of that celebrated master-piece of Rubens, in which he has introduced the portraits of himself and his whole family. The doors that concealed this capital performance were no sooner unfolded, than our enthusiast, debarred the use of speech, by a precise covenant with his friend Pickle, lifted up his hands and eyes, and putting himself in the attitude of Hamlet, when his father's ghost appears, adored in silent ecstasy and awe."

146 Frans Floris de Vriendt (*c.*1516–70)—*The Fall of the Rebel Angels*, painted in 1554, is now in the Koninklijk Museum, Antwerp.

147 Quintin Massys (1465/6–1530) born in Louvain but worked in Antwerp. Note he died prior to the paintings of *The Fall of the Rebel Angels*. The story of him painting the hornet is clearly apocryphal.

Edward Browne noted something similar of his visit in 1668:

"In this Church there is much Carving, and a great number of Pictures highly esteemed, among which one piece is much taken notice of, drawn by *Quintin* at first a Smith, who made the neat Iron work of the Well before the West door; and afterwards to obtain his Mistress, he proved a famous Painter; his head is set up in Stone at the entrance of the Church, with an inscription and this verse.

> "*Connubialis amor de Mulcibre fecit Apellem*"
> Love turned a blacksmith into a great artist

An Account of Several Travels through a Great Part of Germany, (1677).

148 Michiel Coxie (1499–1592), artist of Antwerp.

149 The Town Hall, in the Renaissance style, architect Cornelis Floris de Vriendt, completed 1564. Pieter Snyers (1681–1752) described by Loveday in 1737 as "the greatest Master of Painting now at Amsterdam"—S. Markham, *John Loveday of Caversham, 1711–1789*, (1984).

150 The Jesuit church (now St Charles Borromeo) was designed by Pieter Huyssens between 1615-23 but the design of the facade is attributed in part to Rubens. The interior of the church was destroyed following a lightning strike in 1718.

151 Sir Anthony van Dyck (1599–1641)—after Rubens the greatest Flemish painter of the seventeenth century.
Artus Quellin (1609–68)—the most distinguished of a family of sculptors, born in Antwerp.

152 In 1803 St Paul's assumed the rights of the former parish church of St Walburga which has since been demolished. The altar piece, *The Elevation of the Cross* of 1610 is now in the north transept of the cathedral.

153   The church of St James was built 1491–1656. Rubens's tomb lies behind the main altar in the chapel of Our Lady. The painting referred to is of *Our Lady surrounded by saints*. On each side of Rubens as St George are two women, his wives.

154   Built in 1531 by Domien de Waghemakere it was the first purpose-built Stock Exchange in the world. It was burnt down in 1858 after which the present neo-gothic building was erected. Edward Browne had been more impressed than Peckham: "The Exchange is handsome, supported by 36 Pillars every one of a different carving, four streets lead unto it, so that standing in the middle we see through every one of them." *An Account of Several Travels through a Great Part of Germany*, (1677).

155   According to Descamps the silver statue cost 16,000 silver florins 'de Change du Brabant'—Descamps, J.B., *Voyage pittoresque de la Flandre et du Brabant*, (1769).

156   St Paul's church was originally part of the great Dominican monastery consecrated in 1571. The monastery was abolished under French occupation in 1796. The Rubens *Adoration* is of the Shepherds (not, as Peckham says, the Magi).

Notes to Letter XI

157   In 1631 Rubens received a commission to paint an altarpiece of *The Last Supper* for the Chapel of the Confraternity of the Holy Sacrament in St Rombout's, Mechelen. It is now in the Pinacoteca di Brera, Milan.

158   The triptych *The Adoration of the Magi* by Rubens (1619)—the Madonna's face is thought to be that of Rubens's first wife Isabella Brant.

159   This is the church of Notre Dame au delà de la Dyle. Rubens's triptych of *The Miraculous Draught of Fishes* (1617–19) is to be seen on the east wall of the south transept.

160   *Last Supper* by Erasmus Quellin the Younger (1607–1678), pupil of Rubens.

161   The baroque church of Saint Peter and Saint Paul, designed by the Jesuit Antoon Losson. Paintings by Artus Quellin (1609–68), Pieter Franchoys (1606–54), Michiel Coxie (1499–1592) and others.

162   James Essex shared this opinion—'nothing can be more pleasing than riding through the villages which lay very near together in the road, the Cottages are built with Brick intermixt with stone and some are thatched but the greater part are tiled. The Farm Houses are generally of stone; the doors and window frames of blue Marble and the roofs covered with blue slates. The inhabitants of these dwellings seem to vie with each other in the neat and cleanly appearance of themselves and houses.' *Journey of a Tour through part of Flanders…*, (1773).

163   Jean Claude Gilles Colson (1725–1778), stage name Bellecour—great actor of comedy.

164   *Retour imprévu* one-act comedy by Jean-François Regnard (1655–1709).

165   *mauvaise Honte* = self-consciousness.

166   The famous small, bronze statuette of a urinating boy, the 1619 work of Jérôme Dusquesnoy the Elder.

167 François de Villeroy (1644–1730), marshall of France, favourite of Louis XIV, defeated by Marlborough at Ramillies, 1706, in the subsequent War of the Spanish Succession.

168 The gothic cathedral of St Michael and St Gudula.

169 Archdule Ernest of Austria (1553–1595); governor of Spanish Netherlands, 1594–95.

170 The fire had actually taken place 40 years before—in 1731. Loveday considered the Park "small enough in England to be called a Paddock", Sarah Markham, *John Loveday of Caversham 1711–1789*, (1984).

171 The Palace of Charles Alexandre de Lorraine, governor of the Austrian Netherlands (1741–80). Construction began in 1757, now houses the Museum of the Eighteenth Century.

172 Alavert = Allé Verte.

173 The Hôtel de Ville—a gothic masterpiece of the fifteenth century. The 'fine cupola' to which Peckham refers is the 96m tall octagonal belfry designed by Jan van Ruysbroeck.

174 Probably David Teniers the Younger (1610–90) his output being enormous but possibly by another member of the Teniers family.

175 The Carracci—Bolognese family of painters, late sixteenth and early seventeenth centuries.

176 Adam Frans van der Meulen (1632–1690).

Notes to Letter XII

177 Alost = Aalst.

178 The great church is St Martin's. The St Roch altarpiece is by Peter Paul Rubens although other pictures in the church are from the school of Rubens.

179 Peckham is confused. As St Ann was not martyred it may be that the picture Peckham refers to is that of the martyrdom of St Catherine by Pierre Tyssens (1624–1677). There is in the church a picture (copied from Rubens by Theodor van Thulden ca. 1625) of St Ann teaching St Mary to read.

180 The Abbey of St Pierre was occupied by the French during the Napoleonic Wars when it ceased to be a monastic community. In 1810 it was purchased by the city of Ghent. For a long time it was a military garrison. Restoration work began in 1948 and is now complete.

181 This is probably the picture described by Descamps as being one of the officers of the Ostrogothic king Totila before St Benedict and is by Gaspar de Crayer (1584–1669)—not Croyer as Peckham has it—see *Voyage Pittoresque de la Flandre et du Brabant*, (1769).

182 Elimus was a sorcerer 'full of all subtility and all mischief' blinded by Paul 'for a season'—see Acts, Chap. 13.

183 The reference to the Van Dyck *Crucifixion* suggests that the church Peckham is referring to is St Michael's.

184 For Charles of Lorraine, see Letter XI, Note 171.

185 This would appear to be evidence that these are not genuine letters. It was to be some weeks before Peckham saw the Gobelins tapestries of Don Quixote at Marly-le-Roi (see Letter XVII). However, there is another

explanation. Louis XV ordered a set of thirty tapestries of scenes from Don Quixote for his palace at Marly. In the event he only required 18 and gave the rest to courtiers including the English ambassador (in 1765), the Duke of Richmond. Peckham may very well have seen the Duke's tapestries at Goodwood.

186 The gothic cathedral of St Bavo (St Baafskathedraal), completed 1569.

187 The 'vacancies' were a consequence of the outbreak of iconoclasm which had accompanied the Calvinist Revolution of 1577—see Jonathan I. Israel—*The Dutch Republic: its Rise, Greatness, and Fall—1477–1806,* (1995).

188 The baroque pulpit was sculpted by Laurent Delvaux in 1745.

189 The painting by Rubens is of St Bavo entering the monastery. Peckham makes no mention of the most famous work of art in the cathedral—if not in Belgium—Jan and Hubert Van Eyck's *The Adoration of the Mystic Lamb.* Presumably, the polyptych was closed when he visited on a Thursday so that the full glory of the painting could not be seen.

190 Fiamingo = Fiamningo (Italian for Fleming)—this name was adopted by a number of Flemish artists who had worked in Italy. This Fiamningo was the sculptor Jerome Duquesnoy the Younger (1602–54). The 'boys' Peckham refers to are putti. The artist was executed by strangulation for committing sodomy in church. Again Peckham reveals knowledge of French art which he had not yet seen. He compares Duquesnoy with the great Florentine Michelangelo Buonarroti (1475–1564).

191 The Maison de Ville or Stadhuis—the older, gothic façade overlooks the Hoogstraat; the classical façade faces the Botermarkt.

192 Rather than the coronation of Charles V this may be the picture described by Descamps and attributed by him to Rubens of the abdication of Charles V in favour of his son Philip II—Descamps, J.B., *Voyage pittoresque...,* (1769).

193 Cebes's *Tabula* or table was a Hellenistic work which was often employed as a medium for moral education. The story of Hercules choice describes his decision to follow the path of Virtue rather than that of Vice.

194 The English Benedictine nuns of Ghent were forced to abandon their convent in 1794. Their community was re-established at Oulton, Staffordshire.

Notes to Letter XIII

195 See J. Essex—*Journal of a Tour through parts of Flanders...,* (1773)—plan of boat.

196 See J. Essex—*ibid*—Described the 'Elegant dinner' with which his party were provided, viz:

First course
Beef boiled
Peas stewed
Soupe
French beans stewed
Herrings pickled on Greens

Sec^d Course
Mutton roasted Veal Fowls Soals Veal stewed

Dessert
Apricots—Plumbs
Pears
Biskits–Crumplins
Filberts
Butter—Cheese

'This dinner,' writes Essex, 'was dressed in the Barge and served in as neat and elegant a manner as it could be in the best London Tavern and at far less expence being no more than fifteen pence each person…'

197 St Salvator's is now the cathedral. The statue mentioned by Peckham is very probably that of *God the Father* of 1682; the work of Artus II Quellin (1625-1700). The cathedral visited by Peckham—St Donatius—was demolished during the French occupation at the end of the eighteenth century. St Salvator's was promoted to cathedral status in 1834. By far the most famous statue in Bruges is Michelangelo's *Madonna* in the church of Our Lady. According to Essex, Lord Orford had offered 30,000 florins for it.

198 The cathedral church of St Donatius was destroyed by the French later in the century and St Salvator's became the cathedral. The picture to which Peckham here refers is probably that of St Charles Borromeo giving communion to victims of the plague by Gilles Bakereel—described by J.B. Descamps, *Voyage Pittoresque de la Flandre et du Brabant*, (1769).

199 The English Convent is on Carmerstraat. The beautiful baroque chapel, of which the altar is indeed the highlight, was built in the 1620s.

200 The gothic Town Hall was started in 1376.

201 The 'church' is the Basilica of the Holy Blood (Helig Bloed Basiliek).

202 *The Elevation of the Cross* was in fact painted by Anthony Van Dyck (1599–1641) in 1631.

203 Lisle = Lille.

204 Lille was part of the Pré Carré: the double line of fortified towns stretching from Gravelines to Maubeuge. The walls were demolished in 1858.

205 Rue de Malade—now the Rue de Paris. The gate is the Porte de Paris, built 1685–1692. It also serves as a triumphal arch built to celebrate Louis XIV's capture of the city in 1667. The work of Simon Vollant, it replaced the medieval Porte de Malade.

206 The Market Place or Grand'Place is divided by the Bourse (of 1653) and subsequent building into the Place Général-de-Gaulle to the west and the Pl. du Théâtre to the east. Peckham was staying at L'Hôtel Royal. The royal guard was housed at the Grand'Garde (of 1717) the façade of which still exists.

207 The present cathedral of Notre-Dame-de-la-Treille is a nineteenth century construction. Prior to the Revolution the shrine of N.D.-de-la-Treille was in the church of St Pierre, destroyed in 1793.

208 *The Descent from the Cross* was commissioned for the high altar of the Capuchin church and painted by Rubens 1616–17. It is quite different from the Antwerp Descent. The church no longer exists but the painting is in the Palais des Beaux-Arts, Lille.

209 This altar-piece by Van Dyck is now in the Palais des Beaux-Arts, Lille, as is another of the pictures from the Convent of the Recollets, Rubens's *Ecstasy of Mary Magdalen*.

210 *The Miracle of St Anthony and the Mule* also by Van Dyck—Palais des Beaux-Arts.

211 The Jesuit church of St Pierre (of 1740–43) was destroyed during the
     Revolution.
212 St Maurice—a classic five-aisle Flemish Hallekerke. Many of the paintings are
     by Jacques van Oost the Younger of Bruges.
213 The Church of the Carmelites is St André. The pulpit to which Peckham
     refers, the work of Jean-Baptiste Danezan (1733–1801) of Valenciennes, was
     newly installed.
214 The Citadel to the NW of the old town had been built by Vauban, 1668-
     70. Peckham's walk around the ramparts of this, the greatest of Vauban's
     fortifications, would have involved a distance of 2,200m.
215 The hospital may have been the fairly newly constructed (1738) 'hôpital
     Général' rather than the twelfth century Hôspice Comtesse in the Rue de la
     Monnaie. In reference to the former the painter Jean-Baptiste Descamps who
     was in Lille the year before Peckham refers to 'un beau Tableau, peint par van
     Dyck' representing the Adoration of the Shepherds. Of it he wrote 'la figure
     de la Vierge n'est pas très-corrccte pour le dessein'—J.B. Descamps, *Voyage
     pittoresque…*, (1769).
216 However, when Mrs Thrale was there in 1775 she saw "nothing in it but some
     Rice in one Corner" (7 November 1775—Tyson & Guppy, *The French Journals
     of Mrs Thrale and Doctor Johnson*) and, despite its size, there were grain riots in
     Lille in the spring of 1789.
217 *Le Dissipateur*—a verse comedy, one of his best, by Philippe Destouches [real
     name Néricault] (1680-1754), first performed 1737.

Notes to Letter XIV

218 The church of St Pierre.
219 Not to be confused with the present cathedral. That to which Peckham refers
     was one of the greatest medieval cathedrals of France, completely destroyed
     during the Revolution.
220 The equivalent of 5s sterling at the time—see Appendix.
221 In fact Nonette, a tributary of the Oise.
222 'The King'—Louis XV.
223 A similar point was made by Mrs Thrale. Of the road between Fontainebleau
     and Paris she observed, "Game constantly moving on each side of your
     Carriage as you drive—Hares, Pheasants, Partridges—not now and then
     a few of them to stare at but seen as frequently as Magpies among us, and
     feeding fearlessly by the Roadside"—Tyson M.& Guppy H. (eds.), *The
     French Journals of Mrs Thrale & Dr Johnson …*,(1932) 21 Oct. 1775. Earlier
     in the century Thomas Gray had described the route from Paris to Versailles
     which involved "passing through a road speckled with vines and villas and
     hares and partridges" before arriving at the Grand Avenue (letter to Richard
     West, 22 May 1739—Beresford J. (ed.), *Letters of Thomas Gray*, (1925). Gray's
     friend William Cole, in 1765 saw "plenty of Pheasants, Partidges and hares,
     which grew more common and plentiful the nearer we approached the
     Metropolis"—Stokes F.G. (ed.) *A Journal of my Journey to Paris in the Year
     1765*, (1931).

224 (a) Rue Jacob—on the Left Bank, parallel to and to the north of the Boulevard St. Germain.
(b) According to William Cole, Horace Walpole who four years before had stayed in lodgings at the Hôtel du Parc Royal in the Rue du Colombier had paid 14 guineas a month—Stokes (ed.) *Journal of my Journey to Paris…*

225 Tobias Smollett, in his scathing record of his *Travels in France and Italy* (1766), Letter VI, 12 October 1763, was of a similar view: "Nothing gives me such chagrin, as the necessity I am under to hire a valet de place, as my own servant does not speak the language. You cannot conceive with what eagerness and dexterity these rascally valets exert themselves in pillaging strangers".

226 'two courses of seven and five' i.e. one course of seven dishes, followed by another of five. The custom, known as 'à la Français' in England, was to confine your attention to those nearest to you.

227 Les Blancs Manteaux—religious order founded in Marseilles in 1252. Later—in letter XX—Peckham refers to an earlier visit to Angers.

228 "Christ will reshape everything that you have lost in a manifold and miraculous way at the Glorification of those bodies which in the future will be blessed: and then at last will be proved false the rule of the dialecticians who say that 'that of which one has been deprived can never be restored'."

Notes to Letter XV

229 At this time Vauxhall, the creation of the Italian pyrotechnician Torre, on the Boulevard du Temple was enjoying a great vogue. By 1782 it was open twice a week between five and ten in the evening. The price of admission was 30 sous. It catered especially for the growing tourist trade. Mrs Thrale described the Boulevards as "Places of publick amusement for the ordinary Sort of People & consist of rooms, Arbours, Walks &c. filled with Fiddles, Orgeat, *Lasses and other Refreshments* but no Wine, Beer or Spirits are sold, so there is Gayety without Noise, and a Crowd without a Riot."—Tyson & Guppy, *The French Journals…*, (1932)—entry for 29 Sept. 1775.

230 Paris was the largest city in continental Europe. Peckham's reaction was typically English—"Unless the traveller was a blasé Londoner, accustomed to an even larger metropolis, the scale of Paris came as a shock even to those who had read about it. From the North Sea to the Mediterranean, there was no human settlement so large, although no one knew exactly how large. Guesses at the number of inhabitants ranged from 500,000 to over a million"—D. Garrioch, *The Making of Revolutionary Paris*, (2004).

231 Pont-neuf—constructed between 1578–1607. Despite its name, the oldest bridge in Paris. In fact it has 12 arches. Peckham probably discounted the part of the bridge which crosses the Ile de la Cité. Colin Jones—*Paris: biography of a city*, (2004) describes it as 'the Eiffel tower of the Ancien Régime'.

232 The equestrian statue of Henri IV was unveiled in August 1613. It was destroyed by the Paris mob on 11 August 1792 the day after the attack on the Tuileries but was replaced by a new statue unveiled by Louis XVIII in 1818. Fragments of the original are to be found in the Louvre. Jean Boulogne (1529–1608) was of Franco-Flemish origin but was known in Italy, where he worked, as Giovanni Bologna or Giambologna. The rider was completed in his

studio after his death by Pietro Tacca—Avery, C., *Giambologna: the Complete Scuplture,* (1987).

233 La Samaritaine—so called in reference to the story of Jesus and the Samarian woman from whom he asked for water in John 4, 7-30. The building was demolished in 1813 but the name survived in that of the department store La Samaritaine at the northern end of the Pont-neuf.

234 Pont-royal—'the most modern' bridge had been completed in 1689. The Pont-Mitchel is the Pont St Michel.

235 The young Thomas Gray was similarly impressed by the quays of the Seine. In a letter to Thomas Ashton, 21/4/1739, he wrote 'Along it on either side runs a key of perhaps as handsome buildings as any in the World, the view down which on either hand from the Pont Neuf is the charmingest Sight imaginable', Beresford J. (ed.), *Letters of Thomas Gray,* (1925).

236 Of these gates only the Porte St Denis (built by N.F. Blondel, 1671–74) and the Porte St Martin survive. The victories of Louis XIV gave rise to a degree of military confidence which saw the destruction of a great part of the city's old walls with their fortified gateways and their replacement by these triumphal arches.

237 On the Ile de la Cité—became the Palais de Justice when the Revolutionary Tribunal began dispensing justice there in 1793. The Palais de la Cité ceased to be a royal residence during the reign of Charles V (1364–80) and became the seat of the parliament and various courts.

238 Built to remind Marie de Medicis of her native Florence, being in the style of the Pitti Palace. Since 1750 it had been open to the public twice a week.

239 These enormous paintings—executed 1622–25—are now in the Louvre, the cycle re-assembled as Marie originally saw it. Their creation is brilliantly described in P. Oppenheimer: *Rubens: a Portrait,* (1999).

240 Mr Ricault—probably the portrait painter Hyacinthe Rigaud (1659–1743).

241 Nicolas Poussin (1594–1665) executed two paintings with this subject: this is likely to be the one now in the Louvre.

242 Guido Reni (1575–1642), Bolognese artist.

243 François Puget's *The Musicians of Louis XIV,* painted in 1687, is now in the Louvre.

244 In fact this is Tobias and his family, not Job. The painting is of *The Archangel Raphael departing from Tobias and his Family* (1637).

245 Raphael (1483–1520) executed several such paintings. This is almost certainly the one now in the Louvre, known as *La Belle Jardinière.*

246 'The grand façade towards the river'—including the Grande Galerie, completed in the reign of Henri IV who invited artists to live and work there, a tradition which lasted until ended by Napoleon.

247 chapiters—capitals (Fr. chapiteaux).

248 The quadrangle is the Cour Carrée built during the reign of Louis XIV.

249 By this time the *Salon* was a biennial event. It started on the feast day of St Louis (25 August) and ran for some weeks, so that the 1769 *Salon* would have thus coincided with Peckham's visit.

250 The Tuileries Palace survived the Revolution but was set on fire and destroyed by the Communards in 1871.

251 Nicolas Coustou (1658–1733)—of the family of French sculptors. The statue of the Loire and Loiret is the work of Corneille Van Cleve (1645–1732) and that of the Nile by Lorenzo Ottone (1648–1736).

252 Mrs Thrale's views were similar—"today [1 October 1775] I walked among the beautiful statues of the Tuileries, a Place which for Magnificence most resembles the pictures of Solomon's Temple, where the Gravel is loose like the Beach at Brighthelmstone, the Water in the Basin Royale cover'd with Duck Weed, & some Wooden netting in the taste of our Junketting Houses at Islington dropping to Pieces with Rottenness & Age."—Tyson & Guppy, eds. (1932).

253 Originally the Palais Cardinale.

254 The Galerie d'Enée of the Palais Royal was decorated for the Duc d'Orléans by Antoine Coypel, 1703–1705—Mérot, A., *French Painting in the Seventeenth Century* (1995). This part of the Palais Royal was destroyed in 1784 to allow for the building of the Théâtre-Français. Only three of Coypel's panels and an oil sketch survived.

255 Veronese, Paolo [Paolo Caliari], (1528–1588).

256 Veronese, Alessandro [Alessandro Turchi], (1578–1649).

257 Francesco Albani (1578–1660), Bolognese.

258 Eustache Le Sueur (1616–1655) = *Alexander and his Doctor, c.*1647. This work was acquired by the National Gallery, London in 2000 for £400,000. Originally painted for Jérôme de Nouveau's Paris house, during most of the eighteenth century it was in the Orléans collection. When the collection was put up for sale at the end of that century it was obtained by an English collector. The significance of the subject to de Nouveau may lie in the fact that he was Superintendant-Général des Postes.

259 Correggio [Antonio Allegri], (*c.*1489–1534).

260 Titian [Tiziano Vecellio], (*c.*1485–1576)—his *Venus Anadyomene* of 1520, now in the National Gallery of Scotland, acquired from the Duke of Sutherland but in Peckham's day owned by the Duc d'Orléans.

261 The Bourbon Palace was built for Louise-Françoise (1673–1743), the Duchesse de Bourbon in 1722. Confiscated during the Revolution, it has been the seat of the lower house of Parliament—the Assemblée Nationale—since 1830. The fine neo-Classical facade was not added until 1806.

262 (a) 'the famous Marshall'—presumably Louis-Joseph, duc de Vendôme who defeated Stanhope at Brihuega in 1710, securing the Spanish throne for Philip V.
(b) 'than I to Hercules' in *Hamlet,* Act 1 Sc. ii Hamlet rails against his mother:

        ....married with mine uncle,
        My father's brother, but no more like my father
        Than I to Hercules.

263 Jacques-François Blondel (1705–1774), architect of the Académie Royale d'Architecture; contributed article on Archiecture to the *Encyclopédie.*

264 During the Revolution, when these statues were smashed, the cathedral was re-named the Temple of Reason. The work of restoration began in 1845 during the reign of Louis-Philippe.

265 The huge statue stood to the right of the entrance. Contemporary taste agreeing with Peckham's, it was pulled down in 1785. Cole called it "a great Disfigurement & Blemish to the Church", Cole, W., *A Journal of my Journey to Paris in the year 1767,* (1931).

266 Jean Jouvenet (1644–1717)—the leading French painter of religious subjects of his day. Cole refers to these "8 most ample & glorious Pictures, in Frames of suitable Proportion & Expence". Jouvenet's picture of the visitation was painted with his left hand "under it is wrote this, *Iouvenet Dextrâ Paraliticus, Sinistrâ pinxit*"—Stokes, F.G.(ed.), *A Journal...* (1931).

267 A new high altar had been built under the direction of Robert de Cotte (1656–1735) between 1699 and 1725.

268 *The Pietà* of 1712-28 by Nicolas Coustou (1658–1733).

269 "This knife belongs to Faucher de Beuil, by which Guy hath given to the Church of St Mary the Areas (or open Space) before the said Church, which belonged to Drogo the Archdeacon, for an anniversary service for his Mother" (Translated by William Cole, see Stokes, F.G.(ed.), *A Journal...* (1931).

270 Cole describes the same piece of wood: "a small Peice of yellowish Wood, like Box, only it a little worm eaten…" He quotes the inscription: "Eberardus et Hubertus de Spedona Villa, Servi scilicet Beatae Mariae Parisiensis, per hoc Lignum Fulconi Decano Rectum fecerunt in Capitulo Scae Mariae de Coquestu Antecessorum suorum quem tenuerant absque Canonicorum Permissione" which he translates as: "Everard and Hubert of the village of Epona, servant (or tenants) of the Church of the Blessed Mary of Paris have, by virtue of this Piece of Wood, made over their Rights to Fulco, Dean of the Chapter of St Mary, of which they had by the Purchase of their Ancestors & which they held without the leave of the Canons"—Stokes, F.G.(ed.), *A Journal...* (1931).

271 Peckham heard correctly. The seminary was pulled down so that the west front of the church could be viewed from across the Place St Sulpice. Visconti's Fountain of the Four bishops was not erected until 1844. Jacques-François Blondel (see Note 31 above) proposed that squares be created in front of churches—"nothing being so contrary to good taste as to see most of our churches walled in with rented houses, or surrounded by streets so confined, that they obscure the light and destroy the interesting view that a monument of this sort should provide"—quoted in D. Garrioch, *The Making of Revolutionary Paris*, (2004).

272 Carle Vanloo (1705–1765)—French painter; two of his murals are to be found on either side of the altar.

273 According to Cole (p.248) "This noble Pile of Building was erected by Contribution & a Lottery, & carried to its present perfection by the care & unwearied Diligence of the late rector, Mr Languet de Gergy…" who died in 1750—Stokes, F.G.(ed.), *A Journal...* (1931).

274 The Duchesse de Lauraguais—Diane-Adélaïde de Mailly (1713–1760), had been the mistress of Louis XV.

275 The shells had been given to François I by the Venetian Republic and to St Sulpice by Louis XV in 1745. They are of the species *Tridacna gigas*—the giant clam.

276 The foundation stone of St Roch (St Roque), designed by Lemercier architect of the Louvre, had been laid by Louis XIV in 1653 but the church was not consecrated until 1740. Mrs Thrale thought it better than any church she had seen on the continent—"Amiens alone excepted:—so skilful & so pleasing is the Disposition of the Altars"—Tyson & Guppy, *French Journals...* (1932).

277 Pierre-Louis Maupertuis (1698–1759), naturalist and geometrician and astronomer at the court of Frederick the Great. The church also contains memorials to the garden designer Andre le Nôtre and the dramatist Pierre Corneille although the latter was not erected until the nineteenth century.

278 (a) It was in a hired room in this convent that the political club which evolved into the revolutionary Jacobin Club first met.
(b) Pierre Mignard (1610–1695).
(c) Charles Le Brun (1619–1690)—the monument, to Charles Duc de Crequi, Marshall of France and Governor of Paris ob. 1687, is now in St Roch.

279 Charles La Fosse (1636–1716) who also painted the ceiling of the church of the Dôme.

280 (i) Françoise Lemoyne (1688–1737; (ii) Boulogna = Louis de Boullongne the Elder (1609–74) or one of his children.

281 The convent of the Augustins déchaussés, also known as the Petits-Pères, had been built in 1629 in the rue des Vieux-Augustins, near the place des Victoires. Since 1746 the brothers had been allowed footwear and had become known as the Reformed Augustinians. Van Loo's seven large pictures of the life of St Augustine were painted for the chancel of the church between 1746–55.

282 Nugent put the matter of the foundation of the Val-de-Grâce as follows— "The church and nunnery of Val-de-Grâce were favoured by Anne of Austria, mother of Louis XIV, on the unexpected birth of the Prince after she had been married for 22 years" (*Grand Tour*, vol. 4). Today many believe that Louis's father was Anne's lover Cardinal Mazarin—Levi, A., *Louis XIV*, (2004) .

283 Mrs Thrale was similarly enthralled—"We were then shewed the Val de Grace, the high Altar of which pleased me infinitely, Joseph & Mary statues as large as Life standing on each Side of the Infant Jesus who lies in the middle is exquisitely well performed"—Tyson & Guppy, *French Journals…* (1932).

284 Mignard's painting of the cupola of the Val-de-Grâce was, according to Molière, as attractive to 'skilled amateurs' and 'learned society' as it was to 'our courtiers with the scantiest education'—quoted in Mérot, A., *French Paintings in the Seventeenth Century*, (1995).

285 'the church of the Carmelites'—situated in a narrow lane just off the Rue St Jacques.

286 (a) Philippe de Champaigne (1602–74); Jacques Stella (1596–1657); Laurent de La Hyre (1606–1656); Charles Le Brun (1619–90).
(b) In fact Louise de la Vallière left the court for the convent when she was succeeded in the King's affections by the dazzling Mme de Montespan. She took the veil under the name of Sister Louise de la Miséricorde. Of the occasion Mme de Sévigné, who was present, wrote on 5 June 1675 "Madame de la Vallière, beautiful and courageous as ever, bore herself with notable charm and dignity: her beauty struck all the onlookers …"—Hammersley, V., *Letters from Madame de Sévigné*, (1955) . This picture impressed a number of English tourists including Perceval (1726) and William Drake (1768)—see Black, J., *The Grand Tour in the Eighteenth Century*, (1992). It is now in the Louvre.

287 This was the body of James II who had died at St Germain-en-Laye in 1701. The body was placed in Lord Cardigan's chapel in the English Benedictine church where it remained until the coffin was broken into by the mob during the Revolution, the lead being melted down to make bullets. At

the time of the desecration the embalmed body was said to be in a perfect state of preservation but, having been exposed for a whole day, disappeared and, according to Marchesa Vitteleschi, *A Court in Exile*, was never found. However a body, believed to be that of James, was buried at St Germain-en-Laye in 1824—Hilton, D., *Kings, Queens, Bones and Bastards*, (1998). The church is today number 269 Rue St Jacques, a music and drama school.

288 St Gervais-St Protais has the oldest Classical façade in Paris. Peckham fails to note that the view of the façade was partly obscured by the celebrated elm tree—*l'orme de St Gervais*—"a paltry crooked little tree", according to Cole. It was eventually cut down to make gun carriages during the Revolution and was replaced in 1914.

289 The Jesuits had been expelled in 1762.

290 St Hippolyte is in the rue de Marmousets in the XIII arrondissement.

291 Sainte-Chapelle on the Ile de la Cité. Today regarded as one of the great architectural achievements of Western Civilisation.

292 The Sorbonne was established by Robert de Sorbon in 1253 but the Chapelle de la Sorbonne was, as Peckham suggests, built as a monument to Cardinal Richelieu (1585–1642). The Académie française was established by Richelieu in 1637 and reluctantly took on the role of literary and dramatic censor.

293 By François Girardon (1628–1715)—his tomb of Richelieu is probably his greatest achievement. Cole called it "the greatest Ornament of this Church or indeed of any I ever saw, either here or elsewhere"—Stokes, F.G.(ed.), *A Journal…* (1931).

294 Martin Desjardins (1640–94).

295 The Collège de Quatre Nations was founded by Cardinal Mazarin who, in 1657, commissioned Louis Le Vau to undertake its construction. There is some uncertainty as to what constitute the four nations—Artois, Alsace, Pignerol and Roussillon-Cerdagne are suggested among others. Mazarin donated his library to the college and it was opened to the public in 1691. Under Napoleon the College became the palace of the Institut de France.

296 Antoine Coysevox (1640–1720)—sculptor. The tomb of Mazarin is now in the Louvre.

Notes to Letter XVI

297 Construction began in 1670 and the building was completed five years later. John McManners has pointed out that whilst the Invalides was "a showpiece for the rest of Europe to admire", its inmates were exceptionally fortunate for, with the exception of that foundation, "the government parsimoniously refused to make provision for retired soldiers"—McManners, J., *Church and Society in Eighteenth Century France, Vol. 1*, (1999).

298 The Dôme church was built for Louis XIV by Jules Hardouin Mansard (1646–1708) to a design by Libéral Bruant (1637–1697) as a royal mausoleum. Charles de La Fosse (1636–1716) and Jean Jouvenet (1644–1717) collaborated in the decoration of Les Invalides and the Trianon at Versailles. In 1861 Napoleon's remains were placed in the crypt.

299 *The Glory of Paradise*—St Louis presents his sword to Christ.

300 Ecole-Militaire founded in 1751. Built to the design of Ange-Jacques Gabriel (1698–1782). Its most distinguished graduate, Napoleon Bonaparte, was born in the year Peckham visited Paris. Its construction owed much to the combined energies of the financier Joseph Paris-Duverney (1684–1770) and Mme de Pompadour.

301 The military school at La Flèche was founded in a building which until 1762 had been a Jesuit convent. Cadets are still educated there at Le Prytanée National Militaire.

302 Originated as a dyeworks set up by the Gobelins brothers ca.1440. Became a tapestry factory in early seventeenth century and came under royal control in 1662. Still operating.

303 The Hôpital-général was established by an edict of Louis XIV in 1656—'a complex of ten buildings, including the grim Salpêtrière for erring or lunatic women, the Bicêtre for madmen, and the vast sad Enfants Trouvés for abandoned children.' J. McManners *ibid.*

304 La Halle-au-Blé was built on the site of the sixteenth century Hôtel de Soissons which had been demolished in 1748. It was one of the most striking and admired of eighteenth-century buildings in the city. Arthur Young described it as 'The most beautiful thing that I have seen in Paris'—Maxwell, C., (ed.), *Travels in France during the Year 1787, 1788 & 1789*, (1950). The dome was destroyed by fire in 1802 but it was rebuilt and in 1885 it became part of the Bourse du Commerce.

305 Grosvenor Square, London, laid out in 1695.

306 In fact the Place Royale had been built by Henri IV in 1609. It was re-named the Place des Vosges in 1800.

307 Daniel Ricciarelli, sometimes called Daniele da Volterra (1509–1566), died long before Louis XIII was born (1601). The figure of Louis XIII was by Biard the Younger and was executed in 1639. The bronze statue was melted down during the Revolution and subsequently a replacement was erected. In referring to the 'piazza' surrounding the square what Peckham means is the ground-floor arcade. Cole also compared it with Covent Garden.

308 Louis La Feuillade (1673–1725), marshal of France, notorious for his flattery of the King and incompetence in the field. The statue was torn down by the mob in 1792 and in 1822 was replaced by the present equestrian statue of the Sun King.

309 Writing at the end of the seventeenth century another English traveller had expressed disapproval of the statue:
"Close behind [Louis] is the statue of Victoire, that is a female of vast size, with wings, holding a laurel Crown over the head of the King and resting one foot upon a globe. Great exceptions are taken by artists to the gilding … but what I chiefly dislike in this performance is the *great woman* perpetually at the king's back which, instead of expressing victory seems to act as an encumbrance and fatigue him with her company…" M. Lister, *A Journey to Paris in the Year 1697*, (1699).

310 Place Vendôme—the equestrian statue was designed by François Girardon and cast by J.B. Keller, it was destroyed during the Revolution.

311 Place Louis XV now the Place de la Concorde. Edmé Bouchardon (1698–1762)—celebrated French sculptor, creator of several works at Versailles and at St Sulpice, Paris. By contrast with Peckham, Thomas Jefferson when he visited

Paris in the 1780s was very much taken with this statue as was William Cole. Colin Jones refers to Bouchardon's "masterly equestrian statue of the King", *Paris: Biography of a City*, (2004). It was destroyed during the Revolution. The pasquinade might be translated—"Bouchardon is a brute/His work is pitiable/He puts Vice on horseback/And the Four Virtues on foot." John Moore quoted this and another pasquinade on the same subject—'Voilà notre Roi comme il est à Versailles, Sans foi, sans loi, et sans entrailles' [Here is our King as he is at Versailles—faithless, lawless and merciless]—*A View of Society and Manners in France, Switzerland and Germany*, Vol. 1, (1779).

312   There appears to have been no progress since Cole's visit in 1765. He was told that "the Houses did not let well nor were people eager to take Leases to build on the spot," Stokes, F.G.,(ed.), *A Journal…*, (1931).

313   Jean Dauberval was so popular that the public paid his debts to prevent a contemplated flight to England—McManners, J., *Church and Society in Eighteenth Century France*, Vol. 2. Gaetano Vestris (1728–1808) had been appointed co-choreographer with Dauberval at the Opera in 1761. By 'Mademoiselle Allar' Peckham almost certainly means Marie Allard (1742–1802), the ballerina who was the mistress of Gaetano Vestris and, by him, the mother of the great dancer Auguste Vestris.

314   William Windham, who was also in Paris in 1769, commented favourably on the decoration of the Opera House and the quality of the dancing—Black, J., *The Grand Tour…*, (1992). Of the performers Peckham mentions perhaps the greatest was the male dancer Gaetano Vestris (see note 313 above), according to whom there were but three great men in Europe—"the King of Prussia, Voltaire and myself"—quoted by Mrs Thrale—Guppy & Tyson, (eds.), *French Journals…*, (1932) . Madeleine Sophie Arnould (1744–1802) was a soprano who later created the title role of Gluck's *Iphigénie en Aulide* (1774).

315   The Comédie Française was founded in 1680 by order of Louis XIV, to perform what has become the classical repertoire, in a building attached to the Palais-Royal.

316   Privelle = Pierre-Louis Préville (1721–1799), comic actor and friend of David Garrick. Edward Shuter (1728?–1776) was an English comic actor who played all of the major comic roles including Falstaff, Master Stephen (*Every Man in his Humour*) and Scrub (*The Beaux Stratagem*).

317   The Comédie Italienne: already performing in French when Garrick visited Paris in 1751 and saw a play by Marivaux.

318   This was, almost certainly, Charles-Antoine Bertinazzi (1713–83), known as Carlini. He played the part of Harlequin for many years and was seen by Mrs Thrale in 1775. John Moore wrote of his 'wonderful näiveté and comic powers … which make us forget the extravagances of the Italian drama and which create objects of unbounded mirth from a chaos of the most incoherent and absurd materials'—*A View of Society and Manners…*, (1779).

319   Jean Louis La Ruette (1731–92), actor and composer of comic opera.

320   Madame Trial—Marie-Jeanne Trial (née Milon)—coloratura soprano, wife of Antoine (1736–92) who gave his name to a thin, high, nasal tenor voice.

321   The Cabinet du Roi was later incorporated into the Muséum National d'Histoire Naturelle in the Rue Buffon.

322   Amiantes—a group of fibrous, metamorphic rocks, including asbestos.

323   (1) Antaeus—giant son of Poseidon and Earth, compelled all-comers to wrestle with him, always the victor until defeated by Hercules, who prevented him from deriving strength from his Mother Earth.

(2) Mr and Mrs Thrale, with Dr Johnson and Giuseppe Baretti also stayed in the Rue Jacob and Mrs Thrale wrote in her Journal (23 October 1775)—"… nothing is so false as the Notion of the French Police being so excellent as to prevent disturbance in the streets. I have from my window seen more Quarrels, Overturns and Confusion in the Rue Jacob, where I have now lived a Month than London will exhibit in a year's walking the Street at decent Hours only…"—Tyson & Guppy, (eds.), *French Journals…*, (1932).

Notes to Letter XVII

324 La Muette—a hunting lodge used by the medieval kings when hunting in the Bois de Boulogne, it was converted into a small chateau for Marguerite de Valois, first wife of Henri IV. It had been much modified by Jacques V Gabriel (1666–1742) for Louis XV who entertained his mistresses there—Gallet M & Bottineau Y., *Les Gabriel*, (1982).

325 Francis had become Charles's prisoner after the French defeat at Pavia in 1525. By the Treaty of Madrid the French king agreed to surrender Flanders, Artois and Tournai and give up his claim to a number of Italian cities. He also swore that if he could not persuade the French Estates to surrender Burgundy he would return to captivity. Once back in France Francis made no effort to implement the terms of the treaty nor did he show any inclination to return to the Spanish capital.

326 The Catholic League had been formed to overthrow the Treaty of Monsieur of 1576 which had given the French Protestants—the Huguenots—full religious liberty. Henri had its leaders—Guise and his brother—murdered. He himself met a similar fate at the hands of Jacques Clément, a Dominican friar, after allying himself with the Huguenot leader Henri of Navarre, the future Henri IV.

327 St Cloud was to become a favourite residence of both Louis XVI and Napoleon. It was destroyed by a fire which broke out during the Prussian occupation in 1870.

328 Pierre Mignard (1612–1695)—became Director of the Académie and principal painter to the king in 1690. Supporter of the 'Rubensistes' (as opposed to the 'Poussinistes').

329 This may have been a service of which Peckham himself availed for he left to his daughter by his Will 'such French and English books out of my Library as my Executors may think proper for her to use'—National Archives, PROB 11/1152.

330 Henri de la Tour d'Auvergne (1611–1675), vicomte de Turenne, marshall of France.

331 Ptolemy II, Philadelphus (308–246bc)—when the power of Ancient Egypt was at its greatest. La Coupe des Ptolemées, known at St Denis as 'le grand vase d'agate' is actually made from a single block of sardonyx. It is now in the Cabinet des Médailles, Bibliothèque Nationale. The bust of Tiberius is now thought to be of Claudius—also in the Cabinet des Médailles of the Bibliothèque Nationale. The rock crystal with the engraved crucifixion is now in the British Museum having been sold after the confiscation of the treasures of St Denis in 1793. The weeping figures, standing not on their knees, are the

Virgin and St John. Information from *Le trésor de Saint-Denis* (catalogue of the Louvre exhibition, 1991).

332 Bail—a pole separating horses in an open stable.

333 The three courtyards through which the visitor passes are the Ministers' Courtyard, the Royal Courtyard and the inner, Marble Courtyard.

334 New College, Oxford—of which the Wykehamist Peckham was an alumnus.

335 'the grand gallery'—i.e. the Hall of Mirrors ('Galerie des Glaces').

336 The ceiling decoration of 'The Apotheosis of Hercules' by François le Moyne (1688–1737), covers 480m².

337 See Letter XVI—Note 308.

338 Queen Marie (Lezcinska), wife of Louis XV, had died in 1768.

339 Milo, an athlete of great strength, passing through a forest had seen a tree partially split open by woodcutters and had tried to complete their work with his hand which had become trapped. Thus held he was attacked and eaten by wild animals. The statue, signed by Pierre Puget (1620–1694) and dated 1652, has been in the Louvre since 1820. It took ten years to complete in the artist's workshop in Marseilles before being shipped by river to Paris.

340 Perseus and Andromeda, also by Puget and now in the Louvre.

341 Apollo, attended by the nymphs of Thetis, by François Girardon and Thomas Regnaudin, 1666–1672.

342 Enceladus—the mythological giant who was defeated by Jupiter only after being buried beneath Mount Etna. The sculptors to whom Peckham refers include—Gian Lorenzo Berninin (1598–1680), Jean-Baptiste Tuby (1635–1700) and the brothers Gaspard (1625–1681) and Balthasar (1628–1674) Marsy.

343 Louis-Alexandre, Count of Toulouse, admiral of France, son of Louis XIV and Mme de Montespan (1678–1737).

344 The Petit Trianon had only been completed in 1768, the year before Peckham's visit.

345 The King's hunting lodge at Marly-le-Roy was destroyed during the Revolution.

346 Jules Hardouin-Mansard (1646–1708)—Louis XIV's leading architect was also responsible for building Les Invalides and the palace and chapel of Versailles. The octagon hall was the dining room at Marly.

347 Antoine-François Van der Meulen (1634–1690)—Brussels-born painter, famous for his representations of the battles of Louis XIV.

348 Madame Adélaïde (1732–1808)—eldest daughter of Louis XV.

349 No great surprise that, of more than 200 works of statuary, Peckham should have been attracted by *Venus of the Beautiful Buttocks*. A number of these statues are today in the Tuileries Gardens and one of the masterpieces, *The Two Horse Tamers* by Coustou, is now in the Louvre having been formerly at the entrance to the Champs-Elysée where there are now copies.

350 The 'Machine de Marly' raised water 160m from the Seine at Louveciennes. The machine, together with a system of canals and aqueducts, ensured that by 1683 sufficient water—3800m³ an hour—was reaching Versailles to allow the system of fountains, Les Grandes Eaux, to work at full capacity—Levi, A., *Louis XIV*, (2004).

351 James Brindley (1716–1772)—English canal engineer.

352 St Germain-en-Laye—renaissance chateau with terraced gardens designed by Francini for Henri IV.

353 Mount Calvary—Mont Calvaire, now known as Mont Valerian, Suresnes, mid-way between St Germain and the centre of Paris. Today the site of US Cemetery and Memorial.

354 Saint-Simon was of the same opinion:
"Saint-Germain he abandoned; unique Saint-Germain, with its combination of superb vista and the vast stretches of forest that lie close beside; Saint-Germain with its fine views, trees, soil and situation, its abundance of springs, its lovely gardens, its hills and terraces, its capabilities that might have been extended to include the beauties and convenience of the Seine. There was a city ready-made, whose site alone provided it with all that man could desire. All this, I say, he abandoned for Versailles, that most dismal and thankless of spots, without vistas, woods or water, without soil, even, for all the surrounding land is quicksand or bog and the air cannot be healthy…" Norton, L., *Saint-Simon at Versailles,* (1959).

355 Poussin painted a *Last Supper* for the chapel at St Germain-en-Laye.

356 Such a picture by Michelangelo has not survived.

357 'their ideot King' refers to James II of England who lived there in exile 1688–1701.

358 The garden at Choisy-le-Roi, designed by E. André Le Nôtre (1613–1700), the chateau built by François Mansard (1598–1666).

359 In the year in which Peckham visited France Louis XV commissioned a similar 'table volante' for the dining room at the Petit Trianon from the mechanical engineer Loriot.

360 Charles de Rohan, Prince de Soubise (1715–1787)—Marshall of France, astute courtier but indifferent general. Louis-François, Prince de Conti (1717–1776)—had unsuccessfully intrigued with his master, Louis XV, to obtain the Polish throne. His son was Louis-François II (1734–1814), Comte de la Marche; he was to die in poverty in Barcelona, the last of the Contis.

361 A quotation from Juvenal's third Satire:

> A facie jactare manus, laudare paratus
> Si bene ructavit si rectum minxit amicus
>
> Who, taught from youth to play a borrowed part,
> Can, with a glance, the rising passion trace
> And mould their own to suit their patron's face.

From the translation by William Gifford (1756–1826), in Lowes Dickinson G., & Meredith H.O. (eds.), *The Satires of Juvenal,* (1906).

Notes to Letter XVIII

362 He had not told his 'correspondent' any such thing.

363 Peckham seems to have plenty of confidence in himself as a walker. The following is from the diary of his Oxford contemporary James Woodforde for 28 January 1761:

Peckham walked round the Parks for a Wager this
Morning: he walked round the Parks three times in 26 Minutes,
being 2 miles and a Quarter. Williams and myself laid
him a Crown that he did not do it in 30 Minutes and
we lost our Crown by four minutes. I owe Peckham for
Walking—0:2:6

R.L. Winstanley [ed.] *The Diary of James Woodforde*, Vol. 1, (1996)

364 Mante = Mantes-la-Jolie.

365 Peckham followed the Low Church Anglican doctrine of Archbishop Tillotson
who had inveighed against "the real barbarousness of this Sacrament and Rite
of Religion" and who considered it a great "Impiety to believe that people who
attend Eucharist verily eat and drink the natural flesh and blood of Christ.
And what can any man do more unworthily towards a Friend? How can he
possibly use him more barbarously, than to feast upon his living flesh and
blood?"—*Discourse against Transubstatiation*, (1684).

366 Farmer-general—one of the financiers who bought from the state the right of
collecting indirect taxes such as the *gabelle* (on salt) and *tabac* (on tobacco and snuff).

367 Chateau Gaillon built by Cardinal Amboise (1460–1510), finance minister of
Louis XII. The chateau was partially destroyed during the Revolution.

368 Peckham probably means M. Portail who in 1746 tried to sell his office as
president à mortier for 800,000 livres—see J.H. Shennan, *The Parlement of
Paris,* (1968).

369 Peckham echoes Mr Shandy's words in Book I Chapter XVIII of Laurence
Sterne's *Tristram Shandy*—"Why are there so few palaces and gentlemen's
seats," he would ask, with some emotion as he walked across the room,
"throughout so many declining provinces of *France*? Whence is it that the few
remaining *Chateaus* among them are so dismantled—so unfurnished, and in
so ruinous and desolate a condition?—Because, Sir," (he would say) "in that
kingdom no man has any country interest to support;—the little interest of
any kind which any man has anywhere in it, is concentrated in the court, and
the looks of the grand Monarch; by the sunshine of whose countenance, or
the clouds which pass across it, every *French* man lives or dies."

370 Peckham is presumably referring to the spire above the transept—the Tour de
Pierre—which was destroyed by fire 15 September 1822. Two years later the
construction of the present spire, the tallest in France, began. According to T.
Licquet (*Rouen—its history and monuments: a guide to strangers*, 1840) the lead
was purchased by a printer to be made into type.

371 On the occasion of the visit of Louis XVI to Rouen in 1786 the Georges
d'Amboise bell was found to be cracked. During the Revolution it was melted
down for the making of cannon. According to T. Licquet (*op.cit.*) some pieces
were made into medals bearing the following inscription:

> Monument de Vanité
> Detruit par l'Utilité
> L' An Deux de l'Égalité

372 St Maclou is a fifteenth-century parish church; St Ouen the oldest abbey-
church in Normandy founded in 533AD.

Thomas Frognall Dibdin (1776–1847), author of a *Biographical, Antiquarian and picturesque Tour of France and Germany* (1821) wrote of the windows of St Ouen: "You gaze, and are first-struck with its matchless window: call it rose, or marygold, as you please. I think, for delicacy and richness of ornament, this window is perfectly unrivalled. There is a play of line in the mullions, which, considering their size and strength, may be pronounced quite a master-piece of art. You approach, regretting the neglected state of the lateral towers, and enter, through the large and completely-opened centre doors, the nave of the abbey. It was towards sun-set when we made our first entrance. The evening was beautiful; and the variegated tints of sunbeam, admitted through the stained glass of the window, just noticed, were perfectly enchanting. The window itself, as you look upwards, or rather as you fix your eye upon the centre of it, from the remote end of the abbey, or the Lady's chapel, was a perfect blaze of dazzling light: and nave, choir, and side aisles, seemed magically illumined. We declared instinctively that the abbey of Saint-Ouen could hardly have a rival; certainly no superior."

373 Built in 1630 and consisting of 19 boats it was also equipped with a system of opening to permit navigation. It was replaced by a stone bridge, 150 yards further upstream, in 1829.

374 Peckham is here probably describing the Cours de la Reine of which Licquet wrote (*op. cit.*):
"… this public walk was formed for a walk for the ladies, and is one of the finest in the kingdom; its length is about 674 fathoms. Four rows of large elms form the whole length on the banks of the Seine. On holy-thursday, the *Cours-de-la-Reine* begins to be used as a fashionable promenade, and it may be said that on that day, it has a very gay appearance."

Notes to Letter XIX

375 'Our Ambassador'—was the recently appointed Viscount Harcourt of Nuneham-Courtney (1714–1777), famously drowned trying to rescue his dog from a well at Nuneham.

376 Etienne-François de Choiseul (1719–1785), minister of foreign affairs.

377 Esouen = Ecouen; the castle was built by Anne of Montmorency in the sixteenth century. It is now the Musée National de la Renaissance.

378 The present chateau is largely a nineteenth-century creation.

379 The siege of Barcelona in 1697 by Louis Joseph de Bourbon, Duke of Vendôme.

380 Parson Woodforde's Diary contains evidence of Peckham having visited Stowe, the Capability Brown-designed garden in Buckinghamshire. On 1 June 1763 Woodforde, Peckham and other New College men had graduated and at three the following morning ,Woodforde records, Peckham had broken down the doors of his rooms 'being very drunk' (see Introduction). A little later—'Several of our Fellows went at four o'clock in the morning for Stow and all drunk, some in a Phaeton [Oglander Senr & Cooke], some in a Buggy [Peckham & Gother Junr] and some on Horse-back…'—Winstanley, R.L., (ed.) *The Diary of James Woodforde, Vol. 2*, (1997).

381 Mrs Piozzi (formerly Mrs Thrale) was a champion of Chantilly which she
     visited *en route* for Italy in 1784—'Every trick that money can play with
     the most lavish abundance of water is here exhibited; nor is the sight of
     the jet d'eau, or the murmur of an artificial cascade, undelightful in a hot
     day, let the Nature-mongers say what they please.'—Hester Lynch Piozzi,
     *Observations and Reflections made in the course of a Journey through France,
     Italy and Germany,* edited by Herbert Barrow (1967). The garden at Chantilly
     is said to have been Le Nôtre's favourite achievement—Clifford, D., *A History
     of Garden Design,* (1966).
382 Manage = salle de manège, i.e. riding school.
383 Descendant of the Duc de Berwick, natural son of James II.
384 An outrageous claim. Amiens is the largest and, arguably, the most perfect of
     Gothic cathedrals in France. It is today a UNESCO World Heritage Centre.
385 'the present bishop'—Mgr Louis-François-Gabriel d'Orléans de la Motte,
     bishop of Amiens 1734–1774.
386 Abbaye du Gard—founded by the Cistercians in the 12th century. At the time
     Peckham saw it a substantial part of the abbey was being re-built. Much of it
     was destroyed in 1792.
387 Battle of Crécy (1346) at which the French were defeated by Edward III's
     expeditionary army.
388 Smollett elaborated on Marlborough's campaign in the region. Writing of
     Boulogne, he says—"Bye the bye the common people here still frighten
     their children with the name of Marlborough. Mr B's Son, who was nursed
     at a peasant's house, happening one day after he was brought home to be
     in disgrace with his father, who threatened to correct him, the child ran to
     his mother, crying, 'Faites sortir ce vilaine Marlbroug'. "Turn out that rogue
     Marlborough" Smollett, T., *Travels through France and Italy,* Letter V.
389 Smollett made a rather similar point: "The people of the Boulonnois enjoy
     some extraordinary privileges and, in particular, are exempted from the gabelle
     or duties upon salt: how they deserved this mark of favour, I do not know; but
     they seem to have a spirit of independence among them, are very ferocious
     and much addicted to revenge." Smollett: *Travels...,* Letter V.
390 The treaty of Cateau-Cambrésis (1559) between France and Spain recognised
     French possession of Calais, the last English possession on the continent,
     which had fallen to France in the previous year.
391 Eglise Nôtre Dame—the retable, to which Peckham refers, is the work of the
     Flemish sculptor Adam Lottmann (1628). The church, including the altar,
     was badly damaged when bombed in error by the Allies one week before
     Liberation in 1944.

Notes to Letter XX

392 Utile dulci—from Horace's *Ars Poetica*—'omne tulit punctum qui miscuit
     utile dulci'—perfection is to unite the useful with the beautiful.
393 Which he, presumably, had seen on his previous visit to France to which he
     refers in the first paragraph of this letter.
394 Trans. of quotation in footnote—"Abbot Hildouin was the first to write that
     this bishop, having been decapitated, carried his own head in his arms from

Paris to the Abbey which bears his name: crosses were then erected in all the places where this saint had stopped along the way. Cardinal Polignac was telling this story to a marchioness and added Denis had only found it difficult to carry his head to the first station; to which the lady replied *I believe you, in such things it is only the first step which is difficult.*"

395 'without quarters', i.e. backless.

396 Nobles, clergy and the holders of many offices were automatically exempt from the *taille* as were many cities.

397 Pepin the Short, King of the Franks, 751-768 AD.

398 French visitors to London were often struck by the contrast between the streets of London with those of Paris. Thus François de la Rochefoucauld, visiting London in 1784, wrote: "All the London streets are magnificently wide and accurately planned; all of them have paths on each side for the convenience of pedestrians. The streets are usually quite clean, as the flow of water is excellently managed." Marchand, J., (ed.) *A Frenchman in England 1784*, (1933).

399 bidet = pony (Fr. bider, to trot).

400 maréchaussée = the mounted police force, forerunner of the gendarmerie.

401 The references to Angers presumably relate to Peckham's earlier (first) trip to France mentioned at the beginning of this Letter. Religious orders were popularly supposed to own 'three-quarters of the town'—see J. McManners, *French Ecclesiastical Society under the Ancien Régime: a Study of Angers* (1960).

402 'whore of Orleans'—an unkind, Whiggish reference to Joan of Arc.

Note to Appendix D

403 'A franc etrier'—literally 'at full gallop'. A bidet is a pony.

Index